DIPLOMATIC IMMUNITIES AND PRIVILEGES IN INTERNATIONAL LAW

STUDENT'S GUIDE

GRACIEUX MBUZUKONGIRA

Gracieux Mbuzukongira

DIPLOMATIC IMMUNITIES AND PRIVILEGES IN INTERNATIONAL LAW: STUDENT'S GUIDE

Published by Spines Publishing Platform
ISBN: 979-8-90418-517-6

Spines

To recite Scripture you know full well,

but to interpret Scripture, you don't know well at all.

R. Samuel bar Nahman

ACKNOWLEDGMENTS

First and foremost, I wish to express my gratitude to Dad, who constantly called in throughout the time of this research, finding out about the progress of the book, to whom I say thanks, Dad, for your encouragement.

I equally would like to thank my sister by name Odette for her generous sponsorship during this research, as I pray for more blessings for her.

I wish to equally acknowledge my colleague Prof. Anuttama Ghose of the MIT World Peace University for her review and comments on the first draft; nevertheless, any inaccuracies in the book will entirely remain mine.

Special thanks will go to Mayah Sela in Cape Town, South Africa, who made available to me one of the most important sources of materials referred to in this research. I would like to take this opportunity to thank Aaisha Nazeer, Paula Nanez and Gil Dahan for their support during the publishing phase of this book.

Part of this research was conducted during my stay at the Max-Planck-Institute for Comparative Public Law and International Law in Heidelberg. I therefore wish to thank the Directors Prof. Dr. iur. Armin von Bogdandy and Prof. Dr. Anne Peters for their generosity during my stay at the Institute.

Last but definitely not least, I would like to thank my family for their unfailing support. I will forever remain indebted to them, namely Loic, Ngabo, Maria, Kristina, and Lydia, to whom I dedicate this book.

CONTENTS

INTRODUCTION

Although the status of diplomatic agents has been recognized in history since ancient times,[1] questions related to diplomatic immunity remain among the most controversial questions in international law.[2]

Diplomacy is understood as a means through which a State conducts relations with other States and international organizations.[3] Subsequently, as stated in the preamble of the 1961 Vienna Convention on Diplomatic Relations, hereinafter the 1961 Convention, the purpose of diplomatic immunity and other related privileges "is not to benefit individuals but to ensure the efficient performance of the functions of diplomatic missions as representing States."[4]

Indeed, as explained by Christine Nelson, theories behind the principles of diplomatic immunity and privileges have evolved through various stages. First, diplomatic immunities and privileges were understood under the theory of extraterritoriality. Foreign missions were considered as an extension of the territory of the sending State; such missions were considered beyond the authority of the

---

1. See Preamble, 1961 Convention
2. René Värk, Personal inviolability and diplomatic immunity in respect of serious crimes, Juridica International, VIII/ 2003, p 110
3. See Antony Aust, Handbook of international law, Cambridge University Press, 2005, p 117
4. See Preamble, 1961 Convention

receiving State. However, such a theory was abandoned, and it was replaced by the theory of the king's representation. [5]

The theory of the king's representation seems to have followed the original maxim *legatus regis vice fungitur a quo destinatur,* meaning "[a] diplomat substitutes for the king by whom he is appointed."[6] It follows that if a diplomat represents the interest of the sending State, they should be treated with the same respect due to the King whom they represent and not as individuals.

Nevertheless, with time, the concept of sovereignty of States was more and more understood as deriving its basis not from the king but rather from the people, and diplomatic privileges and immunities theories started to shift toward a different understanding that is a necessity needed for the performance of the diplomat's duties.

Thus, the receiving State should refrain from any activity that could interfere with the work of a given diplomat. This justifies diplomatic immunity and other privileges, neither based on the extraterritoriality of the sending State nor based on the authority of the King whom he represents, but rather by the need to ensure the effective performance of their diplomatic duties.[7]

---

5. Christine M. Nelson," Opening" Pandora's Box: The Status of the diplomatic bag in international relations, Fordham International Law Journal, Volume 12, Issue 3 1988, p 498
6. See Aaron X. Fellmeth and Maurice Horwitz, Guide to Latin in international law, Oxford University Press, 2009, p 163
7. See Rosanne van Alebeek, Diplomatic immunity, in Max Planck Encyclopedia of Public International Law, para 3.

CHAPTER 1

KEY CONCEPTS

It is for pedagogical reasons that a student's guide will be introduced by a chapter dedicated to understanding the basic concepts, as it lays down the ground before navigating through various principles governing the subject matter.

Without claiming to be exhaustive, this chapter gives a glimpse of the understanding of key concepts as they will be developed further in the following chapters.

1.1 Diplomatic Mission

A diplomatic mission could be understood as a foreign diplomatic representation, nominated by a sending State and accepted by a receiving State. Such a mission would comprise the Head of the mission together with his staff and would be established in the diplomatic capital of the receiving State.[1]

The Head of the mission is responsible for all matters connected with his mission. He may, from time to time, delegate some functions to his staff; however, he remains the sole responsible to his government and to the government to which he is accredited.[2]

1. See Ralp G. Feltham, the diplomatic mission, in Diplomatic handbook, Brill, 2004, p 13
2. Idem

Irrespective of the naming, all States afford equal privileges and immunities to foreign diplomats of equal rank. Thus, different types of diplomatic missions are recognized in international relations. Some States would refer to their foreign diplomatic missions as Embassies, while others, mainly Commonwealth countries, would refer to their foreign missions as high commissions. The expression Permanent mission is mainly used to mean a diplomatic mission accredited to an international organization.

1.2 Members of Diplomatic Mission

Article 1(b) of the 1961 Convention defines the expression members of the diplomatic mission as including the Head of the mission and the members of the staff of the mission. Further, Article 1(c) clarifies that the concept members of the staff of the mission shall be given a wide interpretation, and it shall include members of the diplomatic staff, the administrative staff and technical staff, and the service staff of the mission.

However, Article 1(d) indicates that only members of the staff of the mission having a rank of a diplomat shall be considered members of diplomatic staff, or diplomatic agents, and subsequently enjoy diplomatic immunity and privileges of their rank. A better understanding of the concept requires that each of its sub-groups be addressed separately.

1.3 Members of Diplomatic Staff

As indicated above, the 1961 Convention does not define the concept of members of diplomatic staff, generally referred to as diplomatic agents or simply diplomats. Not surprisingly, the 1973 Convention on the Prevention and Punishment of Offences against Internationally Protected Persons, Including Diplomatic Agents, "the 1973 Diplomatic Convention," defines internationally protected persons, but is limited only to the said convention.

Though adopted within a specific context of situations of crimes committed against diplomats, such a definition could be informative on what meaning could be given to the concept in general. Indeed the diplomatic convention in its Article 1(1) a, provides that:

Internationally protected person" means: A Head of State, including any member of a collegial body performing the functions of a Head of State under the constitution of the State concerned, a Head of Government or a Minister for Foreign Affairs, whenever any such person is in a foreign State, as well as members of his family who accompany him

Considering the pivotal role played by Heads of State, Heads of Government, and Foreign Affairs Ministers in international relations, they are always considered high-ranking diplomats and enjoy diplomatic immunity of that rank.[3] This was recognized in the International Court of

3. For details see Sir Arthur Watts, The legal position in international

Justice, saying "Head of State, Head of Government and Minister for foreign affairs enjoy immunities from the jurisdiction in other states,"[4] in the Arrest Warrant case.

In addition, Article 1(1) b of the diplomatic convention provides that internationally protected person status shall be extended to:

Any representative or official of a State or any official or other agent of an international organization of an inter-governmental character who, at the time when and in the place where a crime against him, his official premises, his private accommodation, or his means of transport is committed, is entitled under international law to special protection from any attack on his person, freedom or dignity, as well as members of his family forming part of his household.

The concept of representatives, officials, or agents of a foreign State would be better understood when put in the context of persons who benefit from the provisions of Article 29 of the 1961 Convention, Article 40 of the 1963 Vienna Convention on Consular Relations, and Article 29 of the New York Convention on Special Mission. The

---

law of heads of states, heads of governments and foreign ministers, in 3 Recueil des cours 20, 1994.

4. See International Court of Justice, Reports of Judgements Advisory opinions and orders, Case concerning the arrest warrant of 11 April 2000, Democratic Republic of Cong v. Belgium, Judgement of 14 February 2002 para. 51, however, though foreign ministers would benefit from diplomatic immunity their immunity cannot be compared to the immunity of Heads of State. This difference shall be discussed further infra........ For further details see Steffen Wirth, Immunity for core crimes? ICJ's Judgement in the Congo v. Belgium Case, in European Journal of International Law, Vol. 13 No. 4, 2002, p 879

concept of representative, official, or agent of an international organization shall be construed to cover any person who benefits from such status, either as provided for in the constitutive treaty creating the international institution or in its headquarters agreements and the host State.

Thus, the concept of a diplomat could be understood to mean a State official or a representative of an international organization who is entrusted with the responsibility for representing their State or institution and its interests and welfare, and that of its citizens or subjects in the jurisdiction of another State or international organization.[5]

1.4 Family Members

There is a consensus on the rule that members of the family of a diplomatic agent shall enjoy privileges and immunities as the agent; however, what constitutes a family might cause practical difficulties, for instance, as explained by van Alebeek, cases of unmarried partners or same-sex partners same as cases of polygamous marriages are not treated the same in all parts of the world,[6] or unmarried couples living together.

The first suggested amendment to Article 1 which was to provide for the definition of a family member of diplomatic agents was made by the USA, and proposed that

5. See Elizabeth A. Martin, (Ed.) A Dictionary of Law, 5th Edition, Oxford University Press, 2003, p 149
6. See Rosanne van Alebeek, Diplomatic immunity, in Max Planck Encyclopedia of Public International Law, para 43

the concept be understood as: "A member of the family is the spouse of a member of the mission, any minor child or any other unmarried child who is a full-time student and such other members of the immediate family of a member of the mission residing with him as may be agreed upon between the receiving and the sending States."[7]

India submitted its own proposed amendment according to which: "The family of a member of a mission consists of those persons who belong to his family and are also members of his household,"[8] whereas Ceylon suggested rather that the concept be understood as follows: "By the family of a member of a mission is meant his spouse if any, unmarried children, and such other immediate relatives of himself and his spouse, who are part of his household."[9]

Interestingly, none of the three amendments was adopted; the conference decided not to define the concept in Article 1. However, a reading of these suggestions would lead to a determination of some important elements, namely, a member of the family, part of the household of the agent, and the agreement of the receiving State.

Without defining the concept, Article 37(1) indicates that: "The members of the family of a diplomatic agent

---

7. See Document A/CONF.20/C.1/L.17 United States of America: amendments to article 1, 6 March 1961
8. See Document A/CONF.20/C.1/L.90 India: amendment to article 1, 8 March 1961
9. See Document A/CONF.20/C.1/L.91, Ceylon: amendment to article 1, *8 March 1961*

forming part of his household shall, if they are not nationals of the receiving State, enjoy the privileges and immunities specified in Articles 29 to 36."

The requirement of the approval of the receiving State does not appear in this Article, rather being part of the house hold might be considered the most determining factor as said by Jean Salmon, "[à] partir du moment où la personne est notifiée par l'Etat accréditant comme membre de la famille faisant partie du ménage, il n'y a pas de raison de raison que l'Etat accréditaire objecte." [10] Nevertheless, other factors might not be automatically dismissed, since the receiving State might always use its rights to declare non grata any agent it disapproves.

1.5 Non-Diplomatic Staff

The status of non-diplomatic staff deserves particular attention. It could be submitted that the distinction made between Articles 1(f) and (g) of the 1961 Convention is not helpful. Whereas Article 1(f) provides that the "members of administrative and technical staff" are the members of the staff of the mission employed in the administrative and technical service of the mission, Article 1(g) provides that the "members of the service of the staff" are the members of the staff of the mission in the domestic service of the mission.

A fusion of the two paragraphs would lead to the interpretation of the concept of non-diplomatic staff to be

10. See Jean Salmon, Manuel de droit diplomatique, Bruylant Bruxelles, 1994, p 382.

better understood as comprising members of the administrative staff, technical staff, and service staff. Considering that such a distinction does not result in different treatment regarding Article 37, providing for the immunity and privileges of non-diplomatic staff, which does not make a substantial difference between non-diplomatic staff, such a distinction seems to serve no purpose.[11]

Furthermore, Article 1(h) defines a private servant as a person who is in the domestic service of a member of the mission and who is not an employee of the sending State. A quick reading of this paragraph might lead to the conclusion that there is a difference between the two categories. However, as it will be discussed later, there ought to be no difference between the two. As noted by the Indian representative during the diplomatic conference, the category private servant did not require a separate definition, since it could be covered by the previous paragraph relating to service staff.[12]

---

11. Indeed, during the diplomatic conference, the Israeli representative indicated that: "Sub-paragraphs *(f)* and *(g)* did not draw a sufficiently clear distinction between "administrative and technical staff " and " service staff ". Such a distinction was particularly important for the purpose of the application of article 36. [Current Art. 37] The categories of staff to which those two subparagraphs referred should therefore be defined in greater detail." See A.CONFJO/14 United Nations Conference on Diplomatic Intercourse and Immunities Vienna — 2 March - 14 April 1961 Official Records Volume I: Summary Records of Plenary Meetings and of Meetings of the Committee of the Whole, p 56 para 20

12. A.CONF2O/14 United Nations Conference on Diplomatic Intercourse and Immunities Vienna — 2 March - 14 April 1961 Official Records Volume I: Summary Records of Plenary Meetings and Meetings of the Committee of the Whole, p 57 para 32

1.6 The *Agrément*

Article 4 of the 1961 Convention, which provides for the *agrément,* does not define what the concept is. The Convention just creates an obligation to the sending State to ensure the *agrément* of the receiving State has been given to the person it proposes to accredit as Head of the mission to that State.

In practice, the *agrément* comes as a response to a request from the sending State indicating its intention to appoint a given individual as Head of mission or ambassador and requesting the receiving state to accept the proposed person. Such a request does not have the legal value of an accreditation letter, which is rather a more formal letter issued by the Head of State of the sending State after the sending State has received the *agrément.*

Granting the *agrément* is considered a discretionary act of the receiving state; it is not required to motivate its refusal. According to Article 4 (2) of the 1961 Vienna Convention on Diplomatic Relations: "The receiving State is not obliged to give reasons to the sending State for a refusal of *agrément.*"[13]

In diplomatic law, the *agrément* is generally required only for the Head of mission. In certain circumstances, namely

---

13. For instance, at the time of writing this paragraph, Tanzania had just refused to issue the agrément to the proposed German ambassador, in an interview given to a Kenyan newspaper she said: "Tanzania has rejected my appointment [...] but is not under any obligation to explain the reasons." See Margit Hellwig-Bötte cited by Geoffrey Mosoku, in Tanzania rejects posting of the German ambassador, The Standard, Thursday, September 19, 2013, p 19.

in the case of military, naval, or air attachés, the receiving State may require their names to be submitted beforehand for its approval.[14]

1.7 The *Exequatur*

In diplomatic laws, the French term *agrément* used in diplomatic relations should be differentiated from the Latin term *exequatur*, used in consular relations, of which literal interpretation would mean "let it be executed." [15] As provided for by Article 12 of the 1963 Vienna Convention on Consular Relations: "The Head of a consular post is admitted to the exercise of his functions by an authorization from the receiving State termed an *exequatur*."

The *exequatur* is an official document recognizing an appointed person to exercise consular duties. In practice, the establishment of a consular post requires consent from the sending and the receiving State. That means the sending state must secure both the consent of the receiving State for the establishment of the consular post and the *exequatur* of the person who will exercise consular duties for its consular post to be operational if no diplomatic relations had earlier been established between the two States.

However, according to Article 2 (2) of the 1963 Vienna Convention on Consular Relations, the consent to estab-

---

14. See Article7 of the 1961 Vienna Convention on Diplomatic Relations

15. Aaron X. Fellmeth and Maurice Horwitz, Guide to Latin in international law, Oxford University Press, 2009, p 102

lish a consular post could be implied from the consent to establish diplomatic relations, unless otherwise stated.[16] Nevertheless, the obligation to obtain the *exequatur* remains. Such an obligation will also remain even in the case of the replacement of the Head of the consular post.

A discussion emerged during the diplomatic conference about whether the *exequatur* is required when the consular functions are being discharged by a department within a diplomatic mission. The matter could be settled by accepting that, as a rule, Article 3 (3) authorizes a diplomatic mission to perform functions of the consular mission if it has a department set for that purpose. For instance, a diplomatic mission would not require an *exequatur* to issue passports and travel documents to nationals of the sending State, and visas or appropriate documents to persons wishing to travel to the sending State, yet such duties are usually performed by the consul.[17]

However, when the "consular activities, such as the protection of nationals by appearing before the local authorities, or the exercise of some administrative and judicial functions that [are] governed by the legislation of the [receiving] State,"[18] the consular agent might need to

16. Article 2 (2) of the 1963 Convention on Consular Relations says that: "The consent given to the establishment of diplomatic relations between two States implies, unless otherwise stated, consent to the establishment of consular relations."

17. For this example, see article 5 (d) of the 1963 Vienna Convention on Consular Relations.

18. See A/CN.4/SR.509 Summary record of the 509th meeting, Consular intercourse and immunities Extract from the Yearbook of the International Law Commission: - 1959 , vol. I p. 133 para. 57

produce the *exequatur,* according to the practice in the receiving State.

Thus, when performing acts which would produce legal effects in the receiving State, the officer might be required to secure the *exequatur* beforehand. Otherwise, such a requirement might not be mandatory.

Same as the *agrément,* the grant of an *exequatur* is considered a discretionary act of the receiving State and is not required to motivate its refusal. Article 12 (2) of the 1963 Vienna Convention on Consular Relations provides that: "A State which refused to grant an *exequatur* is not obliged to give to the sending State reasons for such refusal." The consequence of such refusal is that it renders the concerned person *persona non grata*.

1.8 *Persona non grata*

In contrast to *persona grata*, a *persona non grata* is an unwelcome or unwanted person. The term is used to designate a diplomat whose request to be posted in a receiving State or whose continued presence in a receiving State is rejected by that State.[19] Article 9(1) of the 1961 Vienna Convention on Diplomatic Relations provides that:

The receiving State may at any time and without having to explain its decision, notify the sending State that the head of the mission or any member of the diplomatic staff of the mission is persona non grata or that any other member of the staff of the mission is not acceptable. In

19. Aaron X. Fellmeth and Maurice Horwitz, Guide to Latin in international law, Oxford University Press, 2009, p 221

any such case, the sending State shall, as appropriate, either recall the person concerned or terminate his functions with the mission. A person may be declared non grata or not acceptable before arriving in the territory of the receiving State.[20]

Article 8(1) of the draft Articles on diplomatic intercourse and immunities adopted by the International Law Commission at its tenth session provided that:

The receiving State may at any time notify the sending State that the head of the mission, or any member of the staff of the mission, is *persona non grata* or not acceptable. In such a case, the sending State shall, as the case may be, recall the person concerned or terminate his functions with the mission.[21]

Several questions were raised during the debate that surrounded the adoption of the above-cited Article, including which of the members of the diplomatic mission could be subject to the process of being declared *non grata*, or under which conditions such a process could be initiated. *Stricto senso*, only diplomatic agents can be declared *non grata;* however, the term not acceptable after "*persona non grata*" suggests that the Article can be used against both diplomatic and non-diplomatic members of staff. Thus, non-diplomatic staff will be declared not

---

20. The corresponding provision is found in Art. 23 of the Vienna Convention on Consular Relations

21. See A/CONF.20/14/Add.l United Nations Conference on Diplomatic Intercourse and Immunities

Vienna - 2 March - 14 April 1961 Official Records Volume II : Annexes Final Act Vienna Convention on Diplomatic Relations Optional Protocols Resolutions

acceptable.[22] It could additionally be argued that since non-diplomatic staff also enjoy certain diplomatic immunities, it follows that they must be subjected to the possibility of being accepted or rejected by the receiving State.

As to establishing conditions under which such a process can take place, the question was abandoned as practice never showed that such conditions existed. It was agreed to be left to the discretion of the receiving State and that the receiving State was not under any obligation to disclose the reason why a given member of staff of a diplomatic mission had been refused.

Nevertheless, practice indicates that when receiving states resort to such measures, they may, if they so wish, indicate reasons it has declared a member of diplomatic *non grata* or not acceptable; however, such reasons are usually expressed in diplomatic terms, conveying the message of avoiding unnecessary diplomatic frictions.

Reasons for declaring a foreign agent *non grata* or not

---

22. As it was rightfully argued by the Spain representative: "[A] declaration of persona non grata, which in some countries required a decision by the full Council of Ministers, was too formal, too solemn and too complicated a procedure to be applied to a member of the administrative or technical staff or of the service staff of the mission. Those persons were often locally recruited; they had resided in the receiving State before their engagement and would continue to do so after it ended. A declaration that such a person was not acceptable might well result from some minor incident that justified the termination of his services — and indeed, if he were a foreigner, his expulsion — but should not be inflated into a diplomatic incident. See A.CONF2O/14 United Nations Conference on Diplomatic Intercourse and Immunities Vienna — 2 March - 14 April 1961 Official Records Volume I: Summary Records of Plenary Meetings and of Meetings of the Committee of the Whole, p102 para 19

acceptable may vary according to different cases. Indeed such a reaction by the receiving State may be caused by the individual behavior of the agent themselves, for instance their involvement in criminal conduct, or other non-acceptable behavior including interfering within internal affairs of the receiving State or other abuses of the diplomatic status, as it can be a reaction against a given conduct of the sending State irrespective of the good conduct of the diplomat.

For instance, in 2007, the British government expelled four Russian diplomats as a response to Russia's refusal to extradite Andrey Lugovoy to stand trial in the UK, allegedly for the poisoning of Alexander Litvinov[23] who was viewed as an opposition voice against the regime in Moscow. It should be indicated that this "punitive" reaction of the State's agent for their sending State's conduct was not contemplated as one of the reasons that could warrant the use of the *non grata* doctrine; however, States have been resorting to the same.

In another instance, such conduct can be a retaliatory measure against the other State in a reaction to the same conduct, as it is usually referred to as tic au tac. This was the case in 1990 when the US requested the withdrawal of four Russian diplomats following the arrest of a Federal Bureau of Investigation ("FBI") Russian spy. In response, Russia requested exactly four US diplomats leave.[24]

---

23. Jean d'Aspremont, Persona Non Grata, Max Planck Encyclopedia of Public International Law, 2009, para 7
24. Idem para 8

In 2014, following an attempt on the life of an exiled Rwanda army General who was living in South Africa, South Africa expelled three Rwandan diplomats over suspected links to the incident. In response, Rwanda expelled six South African diplomats in reciprocity, as it termed its response a reaction to South Africa harboring dissidents responsible for terrorist attacks in Rwanda.[25]

As it was suggested by the Belgian amendment during the diplomatic negotiations, a person may be declared *non grata* or not acceptable before or after they have arrived in the receiving state. The sending State will have either to recall the concerned person or terminate their functions within a reasonable time.

In the event that a given diplomat is declared *non grata* and the sending State fails to recall such a diplomat, the receiving State may refuse to recognize the person concerned as a member of the mission.[26] Other than losing diplomatic immunity and other related privileges pertaining to the previous status, such a person remains protected under other legal regimes applicable to foreigners. Thus, the declaration of a diplomat as *persona non grata* does not automatically provide for legal ground to expel the concerned person, as it only changes the legal regime applicable to them.

Furthermore, the Convention does not indicate how

25. See World Archives, S. Africa's Zuma breaks silence on Rwanda diplomatic row, 12.03.2014, available on www.aa.com.tr last consulted on 21.08.2023
26. See Art. 9(2) of the 1961 Vienna Convention on Diplomatic Relations

much time could be considered reasonable. For instance, in 1967 at the outbreak of the Six-Day War, Iraq requested the Head of the American mission to leave the country within three days, and that the rest of the personnel should leave within about a week.[27]

27. See Grant V. McClanahan, Diplomatic immunity: Principles practice problems, Hurst & Co., 1976, p113

CHAPTER 2

THE ESTABLISHMENT OF DIPLOMATIC RELATIONS AND DIPLOMATIC MISSION

Article 2 of the 1961 Convention indicates that: "The establishment of diplomatic relations between States, [...] takes place by mutual consent."[1] Considered an expression of State sovereignty, the guiding principle is that States establish diplomatic relations and their diplomatic missions by consent between the sending and the receiving State.[2]

It should be pointed out that though the expression right of legation, (droit de legation, Gesandtschaftsrechts) has been frequently used, as said by Ernest Satow, "every recognized independent State is held to be entitled to send diplomatic agents to represent its interests in other States, and reciprocally to receive such agents, there is no obligation in international law to exercise either right."[3]

The active and passive right of legation implies that both the sending and receiving States have recognized each

1. Art. 2 1961 Vienna Convention on Diplomatic Relations
2. See Holger P. Hestermeyer, Vienna Convention on Diplomatic Relations, in Max-Planck Encyclopedia of Public International Law, para 16
3. See Ernest Satow, A guide to diplomatic practice, Vol. 1, Cambridge Library Collection, 1917 p 175. The same position is further supported by Jean Salmon saying: Un Etat n'est pas tenu d'envoyer des représentants diplomatiques ni de recevoir des représentants permanents, ... Il s'agit d'une simple faculté. » See Jean Salmon, Manuel de droit diplomatique, Bruylant Bruxelles, 1991, p 28.

other as sovereign entities. In practice, the establishment of diplomatic relations signifies mutual recognition of the two States, and in the event that a formal recognition did not take place, either as a result of newly created State or a coming in of a new government, as the case may be, the establishment of diplomatic relations will be considered a *de facto* recognition, that is, recognition as a matter of fact.

In other words, international law considers the establishment of diplomatic relations as an act of recognition between States, albeit in a tacit manner. However, the opposite of such a statement is not necessarily true. Indeed, not establishing normal diplomatic relations does not necessarily imply the non-recognition of a state, much less the establishment of diplomatic missions.

International law does not provide a clear set of criteria used to decide whether a government should or should not be recognized; most of the time, particularly when such a determination is made by the Office of Foreign Affairs, it has been dictated by legal, political, and diplomatic considerations.

However, Maria Aristodemou has cautioned that the test of effectiveness and its application remain a matter of contention, as such a test might rather end up testing whether the government has the physical bind of governed.[4] In addition, the question of recognition of the government in exile might not find an answer,[5] as it will be discussed later. Nevertheless, as indicated by Sir

4. Maria Aristodemou, Choice and evasion in Judicial recognition of government, 5 European Journal of International Law, 1994, p 546.
5. For a thorough study see Stefan Talmon, recognition of the govern-

Hersch Lauterpacht, power effectiveness evidenced by an adequate expression of the consent of the governed could be paramount to making such a determination.[6]

In a nutshell, there is no obligation upon States to establish diplomatic relations with all the States it recognizes as such. Even when such a relation exists, States are still not under any obligation to establish diplomatic missions. It could be considered a right which is exercised at the State's discretion. Indeed, even when no diplomatic mission is established within a given State, diplomatic relations can be handled either by a special mission or by a Head of mission accredited in another State.[7]

2.1 Functions of the Diplomatic Mission

Diplomatic agents are "State officials who are entrusted with the responsibility for representing their state and its interests and welfare and that of its citizens or subjects in the jurisdiction of another State or in an international organization."[8]

---

ment in international law, with particular reference to the government in exile, Oxford University Press, 2001

6. Sir Hersch Lauterpacht, recognition in international law, Cambridge at the University Press, 1947, p5

7. According to article 5(1) of the 1961 Vienna Convention on Diplomatic Relations:" The sending State may, after it has given due notification to the receiving States concerned, accredit a head of mission or assign any member of the diplomatic staff, as the case may be, to more than one State, unless there is express objection by any of the receiving States."

8. See Elizabeth A. Martin, (Ed) Oxford dictionary of law, 5th Edition, Oxford University Press, 2003, p149

Article 3(1) of the Vienna Convention on Diplomatic Relations provides for a non-exhaustive list of functions of the diplomatic mission, according to which:

The functions of a diplomatic mission consist, inter alia, of:

a. Representing the sending State in the receiving State;
b. Protecting in the receiving State the interests of the sending State and of its nationals, within the limits permitted by international law;
c. Negotiating with the Government of the receiving State;
d. Ascertaining by all lawful means conditions and developments in the receiving State, and reporting thereon to the Government of the sending State;
e. Promoting friendly relations between the sending State and the receiving State, and developing their economic, cultural, and scientific relations.

In addition to their usual duties, Article 3 of the 1963 Vienna Convention on Consular Relations allows diplomatic missions to exercise the functions of consular missions.[9]

Article 5 of the same Convention provides that:

---

9. Article 3 of the 1973 Vienna Convention on Consular Relations says that: Consular functions are exercised by consular post. They are also exercised by diplomatic missions in accordance with the provision of the present Convention."

Consular functions consist of:

a. protecting in the receiving State the interests of the sending State and its nationals, both individuals and bodies corporate, within the limits permitted by international law;
b. furthering the development of commercial, economic, cultural, and scientific relations between the sending State and the receiving State and otherwise promoting friendly relations between them in accordance with the provisions of the present Convention;
c. ascertaining by all lawful means conditions and developments in the commercial, economic, cultural, and scientific life of the receiving State, reporting thereon to the Government of the sending State, and giving information to persons interested;
d. issuing passports and travel documents to nationals of the sending State, and visas or appropriate documents to persons wishing to travel to the sending State;
e. helping and assisting nationals, both individuals and bodies corporate, of the sending State;
f. acting as notary and civil registrar and in capacities of a similar kind, and performing certain functions of an administrative nature, provided that there is nothing contrary thereto in the laws and regulations of the receiving State;
g. safeguarding the interests of nationals, both individuals and bodies corporate, of the sending States in cases of succession *mortis causa* in the

territory of the receiving State, in accordance with the laws and regulations of the receiving State;

h. safeguarding, within the limits imposed by the laws and regulations of the receiving State, the interests of minors and other persons lacking full capacity who are nationals of the sending State, particularly where any guardianship or trusteeship is required with respect to such persons;

i. subject to the practices and procedures obtaining in the receiving State, representing or arranging appropriate representation for nationals of the sending State before the tribunals and other authorities of the receiving State, for the purpose of obtaining, in accordance with the laws and regulations of the receiving State, provisional measures for the preservation of the rights and interests of these nationals, where, because of absence or any other reason, such nationals are unable at the proper time to assume the defence of their rights and interests;

j. transmitting judicial and extrajudicial documents or executing letters rogatory or commissions to take evidence for the courts of the sending State in accordance with international agreements in force or, in the absence of such international agreements, in any other manner compatible with the laws and regulations of the receiving State;

k. exercising rights of supervision and inspection provided for in the laws and regulations of the sending State in respect of vessels having the nationality of the sending State, and of aircraft registered in that State, and in respect of their crews;

l. extending assistance to vessels and aircraft mentioned in subparagraph (*k*) of this Article, and to their crews, taking statements regarding the voyage of a vessel, examining and stamping the ship's papers, and, without prejudice to the powers of the authorities of the receiving State, conducting investigations into any incidents which occurred during the voyage, and settling disputes of any kind between the master, the officers and the seamen insofar as this may be authorized by the laws and regulations of the sending State;

m. performing any other functions entrusted to a consular post by the sending State which are not prohibited by the laws and regulations of the receiving State or to which no objection is taken by the receiving State, or which are referred to in the international agreements in force between the sending State and the receiving State.

2.2 Appointment of a Citizen of the Receiving State

During the diplomatic conference, the question of the appointment of citizens of the receiving State was the subject of serious debate. A draft Article 7 provided that "Members of the diplomatic staff of the mission may be appointed from amongst the nationals of the receiving

State only with the express consent of that State." [10] After many amendments were considered, the United Kingdom amendment, the current Article 8, carried the day and was adopted as it is.

According to Article 8 of the 1961 Convention:

1. Members of the diplomatic staff of the mission should, in principle, be of the nationality of the sending State.
2. Members of the diplomatic staff of the mission may not be appointed from amongst persons having the nationality of the receiving State, except with the consent of that State, which may be withdrawn at any time.
3. The receiving State may reserve the same rights with regard to nationals of a third State who are not also nationals of the sending State.

However, practice has proved that such practice has been abandoned. Various reasons might justify such abandonment, for instance, in the event of conflicting interests between the appointing State and their own State, the diplomatic agent might be bound by different legal obligations, including the obligation to preserve the interest of their appointing State, yet such obligation does not in any

10. See A/CONF.20/14/Add.l United Nations Conference on Diplomatic Intercourse and Immunities

Vienna - 2 March - 14 April 1961 Official Records Volume II: Annexes Final Act Vienna Convention on Diplomatic Relations Optional Protocols Resolutions.

way release them from the allegiance they owe to their own State.

2.3 Multiple Accreditations

Articles 5 and 6 of the 1961 Convention provide for the question of multiple accreditations. Article 5 addresses the situation whereby a State accredits one person in more than one State, then Article 6 addresses the situation in which more than one State has accredited one person to represent them in one State.

According to Article 5(1): "The sending State may, after it has given due notification to the receiving State concerned, accredit a Head of mission or assign any member of the diplomatic staff, as the case may be, to more than one State, unless there is express objection by any of the receiving States." Whereas Article 6 provides that: "Two or more States may accredit the same person as Head of mission to another State unless objection is offered by the receiving State."

It could be indicated that the initial draft never had a provision on Article 6; it was suggested by the Spanish delegate as an amendment to Article 5, which was later drafted as a separate Article.

2.4 Size of the Mission

The question of the size of the mission has been left to be dealt with by mutual agreement between the receiving and the sending State. If no such agreement exists, then Article 11 shall apply, according to which the receiving state may require that the size of a mission be kept within limits considered by it to be reasonable and normal, having regard to circumstances and conditions in the receiving State and to the needs of the particular mission.

It is expected that the receiving State should not abuse its right to have a say in this respect by allowing or refusing a different State in a discriminatory manner, considering that the diplomatic mission remains an organ of the sending State. At least Article 11 gives two elements that inspire that attitude of the receiving State, which are the conditions in the receiving State and the needs of a particular mission.

If the first criterion could be considered general in a given receiving State, the second element could be subject to the needs of a particular sending State. It is, however, advised that in the event that a receiving State would opt for the limitation of the size of foreign missions, it should do so in a constant manner and avoid any discriminatory behavior.

2.5 Classes of Heads of Missions

For reasons of protocol, the precedence of Heads of the mission is divided into three classes:

a. That of ambassadors or nuncios accredited to Heads of State, and other heads of mission of equivalent rank;
b. That of envoys, ministers, and internuncios accredited to Heads of State;

c. That of *chargés d'affaires* accredited to Ministers for Foreign Affairs.[11]

In the case of Heads of missions of the same class, precedence is given according to the date either of the official notification of their arrival or the presentation of their letters of accreditation, according to the practice of the receiving state. In either case, discrimination shall be avoided.

2.6 Arrival and Commencement of Function of the Staff of the Mission

The arrival and departure of the members of the staff of the mission, as well as members of their families, and of their private servants, must be notified to the Ministry of Foreign Affairs of the receiving State whenever possible.[12]

In diplomatic laws, no presumption of diplomatic immunity exists, and possession of a diplomatic passport is not considered conclusive evidence of diplomatic status.[13] Such notification may prove useful for expeditious immigration entry formalities upon arrival, thus avoiding unnecessary inconvenience to the agent.

Nevertheless, failure of notification or omission on the diplomatic list shall not result in the dismissal of diplomatic immunity and privileges since such notification is also not considered constitutive of such privileges and

11. See Article 14 of the Vienna Convention on Diplomatic Relations.
12. See Article 10 of the Vienna Convention on Diplomatic Relations.
13. See Antony Aust, Handbook of international law, Cambridge University Press, 2005, p 121

immunity. Further inquiries to the sending State may be needed on a case-by-case basis to establish the status of the concerned agent.

Concerning the commencement of their function, the Head of the mission will be considered to have taken up their functions in the receiving State either when they have presented their credentials or when they have notified their arrival and a true copy of their credentials has been presented to the Ministry for Foreign Affairs of the receiving State or to the Head of State, according to the practice prevailing in the receiving State.[14]

2.7 Notification of the Appointment of a Local Staff

Article 10 (d) of the 1961 Convention creates an obligation to the sending State to notify the receiving State of appointments of local staff. Such notification shall indicate the identity of the appointed person and describe the position for which they have been appointed.

A similar notification shall be given whenever the local staff member is dismissed and no longer serves as a member of staff at the diplomatic mission or as a private servant. In practice, foreign missions are discouraged from employing local staff to avoid any possibility of being spied on.

14. See Article 13 of the Vienna Convention on Diplomatic Relations.

2.8 Use of Flag of the Sending State

The mission and its Head are allowed to use the flag and emblem of the sending State on the mission premises, on the residence of the Head of the mission, and the Head of the mission's means of transport when used by the Head of the mission on official business.[15]

In addition, Article 29 of the 1963 Vienna Convention on Consular Relations authorizes the sending State to use its national flag and coat-of-arms on the building occupied by the consular post and at the entrance door thereof, on the residence of the Head of the consular post and his means of transport when used on official business.

15. See Article 20 of the Vienna Convention on Diplomatic Relations

CHAPTER 3

PRIVILEGES AND IMMUNITIES OF DIPLOMATIC STAFF

3.1 Facilitation in the Acquisition of Premises and Accommodation

The receiving State has an obligation to facilitate the sending State in obtaining premises for its diplomatic mission, accommodation for the staff of the mission, and other facilities needed for the performance of the function of the mission.

However, the obligation to facilitate is interpreted as a mere obligation of conduct without being obliged to ensure any result. Further, whenever such facilities have been obtained, it is upon the sending State to provide financial means to acquire them.

Though Article 25 of the 1961 Convention does not define what could be understood as full facilities, such a concept could be given a wide interpretation and should include office supplies and furniture both for the mission and for the staff of the mission.

3.2 Inviolability of the Premises of Diplomatic Missions

As a matter of States practice, the principle of inviolability of the premises of foreign diplomatic missions and representations is embedded in Article 22 of the 1961

Convention, according to which: "The premises of the mission shall be inviolable. The agents of the receiving State may not enter them, except with the consent of the head of the mission."[1]

This provision, which is considered part of international customary law, creates a double-folded obligation upon the receiving State. A negative obligation, that is, an obligation upon the receiving State to refrain from entering such premises.

Indeed, under no circumstances can the agents of the receiving State enter the premises of a foreign mission, except with the consent of the Head of the mission. The fact that amendments proposing an exception in case of emergency during the diplomatic conference were rejected[2] may lead to the conclusion on the absolute nature of the rule.

Further, the same prescription creates a positive obligation upon the receiving State, that is, the receiving State is

1. See Article 22(1) of the Vienna Convention on Diplomatic Relations
2. Such amendments included the Mexico amendment, according to which: "The head of the mission shall co-operate with the local authorities in case of fire, epidemic or other extreme emergency." See Document A/CONF.20/C.1/L.129. Whereas Ireland and Japan suggested "This article shall not prevent the receiving State from taking such measures as are essential for the protection of life and property in exceptional circumstances of public emergency or danger. " See Document A/CONF.20/C.1/L.163 Spain suggested " In case of danger to the life or property of subjects of the receiving State, the local authorities shall address an urgent request for permission to enter the premises and site to the head of the mission, who shall grant such permission unless he takes full responsibility on behalf of his government for the consequences of refusal. See Document A/CONF.20/C.1/L.168

expected to take all necessary measures to ensure a third party does not make any intrusion within such premises.

3.3 Protection from Intrusion by the State's Agents

As said by Hestermeyer, the inviolability of the mission is most stringently confirmed in practice, amongst other things, it prevents service of process.[3] However, the records indicate the existence of cases of violation of such a rule.

For instance, in the DRC v. Uganda case. Indeed, in the case concerning armed activities on the territory of the Congo (Democratic Republic of the Congo v. Uganda) at the International Court of Justice.

In this case, Uganda claimed in its second counter-claim that Congolese armed forces carried out attacks on the Ugandan Embassy in Kinshasa and confiscated property belonging to the Government of Uganda, Ugandan diplomats, and Ugandan nationals; and mistreated diplomats and other Ugandan nationals present on the premises of the mission.[4] Uganda further claimed that the Congolese army also occupied the Chancery and the official residence of the Ugandan Ambassador.[5]

---

3. Holger P Hestermeyer, Vienna Convention on Diplomatic Relations (1961), Max Planck Encyclopedia of Public International Law, 2009, para 25
4. International Court of Justice, Case concerning Armed Activities on the territory of the Congo, (Democratic Republic of the Congo v. Uganda) Judgment of 19 December 2005, para 306
5. See para 309

The International Court of Justice found that, as regards the attacks on Uganda's diplomatic premises in Kinshasa, the DRC had breached its obligations under Article 22 of the Vienna Convention on Diplomatic Relations.[6] Further, the Court explained that it was indeed not necessary for the Court to make a determination as to who might have removed the property reported missing.

3.4 Protection from Intrusion by a Third Person

In addition to the negative obligation upon the receiving State to refrain from violating the premises of the diplomatic mission, the 1961 Convention creates a positive obligation on the receiving State to take all appropriate measures to prevent intrusions or damages to the diplomatic mission by others.

Indeed, Article 22(2) stipulates that: "The receiving State is under a special duty to take all appropriate steps to protect the premises of the mission against any intrusion or damage and to prevent any disturbance of the peace of the mission or impairment of its dignity."[7]

Nevertheless, there is no shortage of examples of violations of this obligation. For instance, during a demonstration that took place on 4. 11. In 1979, the United States Embassy compound in Tehran was overrun by a strong-armed group of several hundred people. The Iranian security personnel present at the Embassy are reported to

6. See para 337
7. Article 22(2) of the 1961 Convention

have disappeared from the scene without making any effort to prevent the demonstrators from seizing the Embassy's premises. After having invaded the Embassy by force, the militant group seized the other buildings, including the various residences, on the Embassy compound. [8]

In the course of the attack, all the diplomatic and consular personnel and other persons present on the premises were seized as hostages and detained in the Embassy compound. Subsequently, other United States personnel and one United States private citizen seized elsewhere in Tehran were brought to the compound and added to the number of hostages.[9]

A day after the seizure of the Embassy, on 5. 11. In 1979, the United States consulates in Tabriz and Shiraz were also seized; however, operations of these consulates were later suspended, and no United States personnel were seized on these premises.[10]

The reason that led to the attack on the diplomatic and consular mission in Iran was explained by Ayatollah Khomeini in his address of 5. 11. 1979, as he said that it was a result of the resentment among the Iranian population against the former Shah for his alleged misdeeds, and against the United States Government which had supported him when he was in power and the decision of

8. See International Court of Justice, Report of Judgments, Advisory opinions and orders, Case concerning United States Diplomats and Consular Staff in Tehran, (United States of America v. Iran), Judgment of 24 May 1980, para. 17
9. See para 17
10. See para 19

the United States to admit him in her territory after the former Shah was evicted from power and the refusal of said Government to extradite the Shah for prosecution in Iran.[11]

The case at hand presents its uniqueness in the thin line that exists between the negative and the positive obligation upon the receiving State with respect to Article 22 of the 1961 Vienna Convention on Diplomatic Relations.

Indeed, the International Court of Justice made a finding that when Iranian militants executed the attack on the United States Embassy, they had no form of official status from which they could be considered as agents or organs of the Iranian State when the attack started. This led the Court to say that the conduct of the militants could not be considered directly imputable to the Iranian State.[12]

However, the nature of the link between the militia and the State of Iran became ambiguous when on 17. 11. 1979, when the Ayatollah Khomeini declared that the premises of the United States Embassy and the hostages were to remain as they were until the United States hands over the former Shah for trial and returns his property to Iran.[13]

First, the Ayatollah Khomeini requested the militants holding the hostages to hand over the "blacks and the women," if it is proven that they did not spy, to the Ministry of Foreign Affairs, so that they may be immedi-

11. See para 88
12. See para 58.
13. See para 73

ately expelled from Iran raises concerns about whether no link existed between the militants and the State.

Secondly, the Iranian Government declared that the noble Iranian nation will not permit the release of the rest of the hostages until the American government acts according to the wishes of the Iranian nation.[14]

Thirdly, on 6.05. In 1980, the Minister for Foreign Affairs, Mr. Ghotbzadeh, is reported to have said in a television interview that the occupation of the United States Embassy had been "done by our nation." Indeed, whereas there were many occasions on which Iranian State officials acknowledged the attack on the embassy as theirs, no record was shown where the same officials either disapproved or condemned the attack.

Although such a statements alone would still not be sufficient to establish the link between the militants and the State beyond reasonable doubt, the approval of The Ayatollah Khomeini and other organs of the Iranian State, lead the ICJ to says that the militia had become agents of the State, at least de facto, as such acts were part of the policy of the Iranian Government. The court thus found that the State of Iran was to be held responsible for acts committed by Iranian militants.[15]

It should be indicated that the absolute nature of this prescription cannot be replicated in consular missions. Indeed, Article 31 (2) of the 1963 Vienna Convention on Consular Relations *in fine* provides that: "The consent of

---

14. See para 73
15. See para 74

the Head of the consular post may, however, be assumed in case of fire or other disaster requiring prompt protective action."

3.5 Diplomatic Courier and Diplomatic Bag

The 1961 Convention does not define the expressions diplomatic courier or diplomatic bag. However, the International Law Commission in its draft Articles on the status of the diplomatic courier and diplomatic bag defines the diplomatic courier as a person duly authorized by the sending State, either regularly or for a special occasion as a courier ad hoc, either as a diplomatic courier within the meaning of the Vienna Convention on Diplomatic Relations of 18 April 1961; or as a consular courier within the meaning of the Vienna Convention on Consular Relations of 24 April 1963; or as a courier of a permanent mission, a permanent observer mission, a delegation or an observer delegation within the meaning of the Vienna Convention on the Representation of States in Their Relations with International Organizations of a Universal Character of 14 March 1975.[16]

Whereas the concept of a diplomatic bag is defined as:

16. Article 3(2) of the Draft Articles on the Status of the Diplomatic Courier and the Diplomatic Bag Not Accompanied by Diplomatic Courier and Draft Optional Protocols 1989, the text was adopted by the International Law Commission at its forty-first session, in 1989, and submitted to the General Assembly as a part of the Commission's report covering the work of that session

The packages containing official correspondence, documents, or Articles intended exclusively for official use, whether accompanied by diplomatic courier or not, which are used for the official communications referred to in Article I and which bear visible external marks of their character as:

a. a diplomatic bag within the meaning of the Vienna Convention on Diplomatic Relations of 18 April 1961;
b. a consular bag within the meaning of the Vienna Convention on Consular Relations of 24 April 1963; or
c. a bag of a permanent mission, a permanent observer mission, a delegation, or an observer delegation within the meaning of the Vienna Convention on the Representation of States in Their Relations with International Organizations of a Universal Character of 14 March 1975.[17]

The purpose of the institutionalization of the diplomatic courier and diplomatic bag is to ensure unhindered communication between the sending State and its diplomatic mission or consular posts, as well as its various delegations wherever they are discharging their official duties.

Thus, Article 27 provides that the diplomatic bag shall not be opened or detained.[18] Further, the packages constituting the diplomatic bag must bear visible external

---

17. Idem
18. Article 27(3) 1961 Convention

marks of their character and may contain only diplomatic documents or Articles intended for official use.[19]

As indicated in the ICL Articles, it is the duty of the sending State to ensure that the privileges and immunities accorded to its diplomatic courier and diplomatic bag are not used in a manner incompatible with the object and purpose of the present Articles.[20]

As for the diplomatic courier, they shall be provided with an official document indicating their status and the number of packages constituting the diplomatic bag, and they shall be protected by the receiving State in the performance of their duties. They enjoy person inviolability, and they shall not be liable to any form of arrest or detention.[21]

3.6 Privileges and Immunities of the Courier

When performing their official duties, the couriers enjoy certain facilities in transit and within the receiving State. Thus, it is expected that such States will allow entry into their territories, and if the courier needs any visa, it shall be granted promptly. Furthermore, whenever possible, if the courier requests assistance in obtaining temporary

19. Article 27(4) 1961 Convention
20. Article 5(1) of the Draft Articles on the Status of the Diplomatic Courier and the Diplomatic Bag Not Accompanied by Diplomatic Courier and Draft Optional Protocols 1989, the text was adopted by the International Law Commission at its forty-first session, in 1989, and submitted to the General Assembly as a part of the Commission's report covering the work of that session
21. VCDR article 27(5)

accommodation or in establishing contact with the sending State or its mission, the receiving State is expected to offer such assistance to the courier.[22]

As for their immunity, the courier enjoys inviolability and shall not be liable for any form of arrest or detention. Indeed, the courier shall enjoy immunity from criminal jurisdiction with respect to acts performed in the exercise of their duties. As long as they enjoy immunity, no measures of execution may be taken in respect of the diplomatic courier; they are not obliged to give evidence as a witness on matters connected with the exercise of their functions. [23]

Indeed, unless there are serious grounds to believe that the courier's baggage contains Articles which are not for personal use, for instance, Articles prohibited by importation or exportation laws, such personal baggage shall be exempted from inspection. [24] However, even when such an inspection is warranted, it should always be carried out in the presence of the diplomatic courier.

As indicated earlier, the diplomatic courier enjoys privileges and immunities for the purposes of facilitating the smooth performance of their duties. It then follows that after the delivery of the consignment, they carry such immunities and privileges should end. However, in practice, privileges and immunities end when the diplomatic courier leaves the receiving State or the State of transit. If the diplomatic courier decides to stay in the receiving

22. Article 14 ICL Draft
23. Article 18 ICL Draft
24. Article 20 ICL Draft

State, their privileges and immunity shall end at a reasonable time that, under normal circumstances, they could have needed to leave.

As discussed in the previous chapter, international law does not define the term reasonable time; each case is to be decided upon taking into account objective criteria, for instance, the facilities available in terms of means of transport, as well as subjective factors, including personal circumstances, physical abilities, health conditions, etc.

If the captain of a ship or the aircraft in commercial service has been entrusted with a diplomatic bag, the sending State shall provide the captain with all documentation indicating the number of packages constituting the bag he carries and the receiving State shall allow a member of the sending State to have unhindered access to the ship or the aircraft to take possession of the bag directly from the captain. Thus, under no circumstances shall the diplomatic bag be left under the authority of the receiving State. It is important to note that diplomatic laws do not grant any particular status to the captain carrying a diplomatic bag.

3.7 Abuses of the Diplomatic Bag

One of the most unsettled questions in diplomatic law is the question of the abuse of diplomatic bags. Such abuses could range from the smuggling of narcotics, weapons, and contraband to the abduction of individuals.

Indeed, in the Dikko case, Mr. Umaru Dikko was abducted at his residence in London on 05.07.1984. As the British security apparatus was on high alert after the abduction, mounting a close watch on ports and airports, customs officials at Stansted Airport became suspicious of two wooden crates from which emanated a strong medical smell as the two crates were about to be loaded aboard a Nigerian Airways cargo aircraft.

Although the two wooden crates had been declared diplomatic bags by the Nigerian High Commission authorities and were addressed to the Ministry of External Affairs in Lagos, they did not have a diplomatic marking on them as required by Article 27(4). At the end, the crates were inspected in the presence of an attaché at the Nigerian High Commission, and two men were found in the two crates, one Israeli citizen and one Nigerian Diplomat.[25]

The 1961 Convention seems to have adopted a firm stand in its prescription as far as inviolability of diplomatic bags is concerned, thus providing for no exception even in extreme situations which could compromise the interest of receiving States, indeed, its Article 27(3) simply provides that the diplomatic bag shall not be opened or detained. This stands in contrast, for instance, with Article 36(2), according to which:

The personal baggage of a diplomatic agent shall be exempt from inspection unless there are serious grounds for presuming that it contains Articles not covered by the exemptions mentioned in paragraph 1 of this Article, or Articles the import or export of which is prohibited by the

25. Adeoye Akinsanya, The Dikko Affair and Anglo-Nigerian Relations, The International and Comparative Law Quarterly, No 3, Vol 34, 1985, p 602

law or controlled by the quarantine regulations of the receiving State. Such inspection shall be conducted only in the presence of the diplomatic agent or of his authorized representative.

As said by Matthias Herdegen, the rigidity of the 1961 Convention, as well as the obvious reciprocal benefits for the sending and the receiving States, have substantially contributed to preserving respect for the immunities and privileges under the Convention.[26] However, the dilemma resulting from frequent cases of abuse has led to a debate on how best such a situation could be handled.

Thus, various alternative methods have been suggested, including subjecting the bag to metal detectors, electronic scanning, or canine sniffing without opening or detaining the bag.[27] Nevertheless, even such methods do not achieve unanimity, as some regard electronic scanning as a "constructive opening."[28] Indeed, the Draft Articles of the International Law Commission in their Article 28(1) suggest that: The diplomatic bag shall be inviolable wher-

26. Matthias Herdegen, The Abuse of Diplomatic Privileges and Countermeasures not Covered by the Vienna Convention on Diplomatic Relations, Some Observations in the Light of Recent Experience, Max-Planck-Institut für ausländisches öffentliches Recht und Völkerrecht, 1986, p 735
27. Christine M. Nelson, "Opening Pandora's Box: The Status of the Diplomatic Bag in International Relations, Fordham International Law Journal, Volume 12, Issue 3, 1988, p 494
28. See Higgins, The Abuse of Diplomatic Privileges and Immunities: Recent United Kingdom Experience, 79 American Journal of International Law, 641, 647 (1985). As cited by Christine M. Nelson, " Opening Pandora's Box: The Status of the Diplomatic Bag in International Relations, Fordham International Law Journal, Volume 12, Issue 3, 1988, p 494

ever it may be; it shall not be opened or detained and shall be exempt from examination directly or through electronic or other technical devices.

Article 35(3) of the 1963 Vienna Convention on Consular Relations provides that:

The consular bag shall be neither opened nor detained. Nevertheless, if the competent authorities of the receiving State have serious reason to believe that the bag contains something other than the correspondence, documents, or Articles referred to in paragraph 4 of this Article, they may request that the bag be opened in their presence by an authorized representative of the sending State. If this request is refused by the authorities of the sending State, the bag shall be returned to its place of origin.

Although the 1961 Convention does not have a similar provision, when the receiving State is faced with a situation that threatens human life or national security, it might resort to the same formula; although there is no unanimity on this suggestion, it is still a viable solution to consider.

3.8 Diplomatic Immunities and Privileges of Non-Diplomatic Staff

Article 37 of the 1961 Convention offers legal ground for immunities and privileges enjoyed by non-diplomatic personnel who are employed by a foreign mission. In simple terms, any individual who is employed by a foreign mission but who does not have the status of a diplomat is considered a non-diplomatic staff member.

As per Article 37(2), such staff includes members of the administrative and technical staff of the mission together with members of their families forming part of their respective households. In international law, such staff are entitled to immunities and privileges for any acts they perform in their official capacities. However, such immunities and privileges will not apply to non-diplomatic staff who are either permanent residents or who are nationals of the host State.

Perhaps this will be another justification for a given foreign mission to be discouraged to employ any staff who is either a permanent resident or citizen of the host State, for fear of an eventual situation where they might be exposed to interference of the host State. Indeed Article 37(3) provides that:

Members of the service staff of the mission who are not nationals of or permanently resident in the receiving State shall enjoy immunity in respect of acts performed in the course of their duties, exemption from dues and taxes on the emoluments they receive by reason of their employment, and the exemption contained in Article 33.

Much that immunities and privileges of the private servant of members of the mission might be reduced, as Article 37 provides that such servants may enjoy privileges and immunities only to the extent admitted by the receiving State. The receiving State must exercise its jurisdiction over those persons in such a manner as not to interfere with the performance of the functions of the mission. Furthermore, they equally enjoy exemption from dues and taxes on the emoluments they receive by reason of their employment.[29] As for taxes and emoluments, private servants enjoy exemptions on the same as would other members of the staff of the mission.

29. For further comment, see Lisa Rodgers, The inviolability of diplomatic agents in the context of employment, in Diplomatic law in a new millennium, Oxford University Press, 2017

CHAPTER 4

DIPLOMATIC ASYLUM

4.1 The Concept

Article 1 of the 1954 Caracas Convention on diplomatic asylum provides that asylum granted in legations, war vessels, military camps, or aircraft, to persons being sought for political reasons or for political offenses shall be respected by the territorial State in accordance with the provisions of the Convention.

Although the Convention does not define the concept of diplomatic asylum, it gives indications that could lead to its understanding. For instance, in Article 3, the Convention stipulates that:

It is not lawful to grant asylum to persons who, at the time of requesting it, are under indictment or on trial for common offenses or have been convicted by competent regular courts and have not served the respective sentence, nor to deserters from land, sea, and air forces, save when the acts giving rise to the request for asylum, whatever the case may be, are clearly of a political nature.

As said by Prakash Sinha, diplomatic asylum is the asylum that a State grants to a fugitive in its embassy or legation situated within the territory of another State.[1] Indeed, one may understand the concept of diplomatic

1. S. Prakash Sinha, Diplomatic Asylum, Asylum in international law, Martinus Nijhoff, p 207

asylum as an asylum granted by a foreign State to a fugitive within its diplomatic missions, which are themselves situated in a foreign territory. As provided for by the Convention, the diplomatic asylum can also be offered in war vessels or military aircraft that may be temporarily in shipyards, provided the beneficiary is sought for political crimes.

Indeed, the 1928 Havana Convention on Asylum, in its Article 1(1) stipulates that: "It is not permissible for States to grant asylum in legations, warships, military camps or military aircraft, to persons accused or condemned for common crimes, or to deserters from the army or navy."[2] Thus, the 1928 Havana Convention suggests that persons accused of or condemned for common crimes who would have been granted protection in any of the places mentioned above shall be surrendered upon request of the local government.[3]

4.2 Historical Development

The practice of diplomatic asylum took root at a time when foreign missions were considered part of the extra territory of the sending State. Indeed, it is recorded that the Statute of Venice of 1554 provided that „he who has taken refuge in the house of a diplomat shall not be

---

2. The same has been referred to in the dissenting opinion of Judge Alvarez in the case International Court of Justice, Asylum Case, Colombia v. Peru, Judgment of 20.11.1950 p 29, saying there is a general agreement that asylum shall be granted only to political offenders and not to persons guilty or accused of having committed common crimes.
3. Article 1 para 2

followed there, and his pursuers are to feign ignorance of his presence.„[4] Whereas it is equally recorded that Charles the Fifth stated that: „May the houses of ambassadors provide inviolable asylum, as did the temples of the gods formerly, and may no one be permitted to violate this asylum on any pretext whatever.“[5]

As said by Alina Malinowska, the concept of diplomatic asylum developed in Europe and was based on the "sanctity" of some places, like churches or embassies. However, later, it was based on the extraterritoriality of diplomatic missions, which were considered as parts of the territory of the sending State.[6]

As seen with the above-cited examples, like most principles of international law, the practice of diplomatic asylum may have started in Europe, though it later gained popularity and was frequently practiced in Latin America, where it became regulated and can be considered part of regional international law.[7] In his dissenting opinion, Judge Alvarez in the Columbia v. Peru case indicates that diplomatic asylum has been practiced in

4. Daru, Histoire de Venise, vol. VI, background documents, p. 83, quoted in Egidio Reale, "Le droit d'asile," Recueil des cours de l'Académie de droit international, 1938, vol. I, p. 513, as cited by the Report of the Secretary-General prepared pursuant to operative paragraph 2 of the General Assembly Resolution 3321 (XXIX)
5. Cérémon diplomatique du droit des gens, vol. I, pp. 480-482 as cited by the Report of the Secretary-General prepared pursuant to operative paragraph 2 of the General Assembly Resolution 3321 (XXIX)
6. Alina Malinowska, The institution of diplomatic asylum as the possibility of protecting human rights, EJIL,
7. Several international instruments have been adopted within the region, including the 1928 Havana Convention, the 1933 Montevideo Convention, the 1939 Montevideo treaty, etc…

Europe, but since the middle of the 19th century, it is especially the countries of Latin America that have resorted to such practice, following the rise of revolutionary movements and civil wars in some countries in Latin America.[8]

Nevertheless, much as it was accepted in principle as part of international law then, history has no shortage of examples of violations of diplomatic asylum. For instance, the report of the Secretary-General prepared pursuant to operative paragraph 2 of General Assembly resolution 3321 (XXIX), amongst other cases, indicates that in 1540 the Republic of Venice used threats to demand the surrender of some magistrates of the Republic who were accused of high treason and who had found refuge in the French Embassy in Venice. Further, England in 1609 secured the surrender of a chaplain accused of high treason who had taken refuge with the Venetian Ambassador to London, etc...[9]

In the first case, it is noted that the claiming State submitted that the Republic of Venice claimed that asylum was not to be granted for the crime of treason. This raises the question of who is competent to assess the criteria that need to be met for such asylum to be granted, a question which, amongst others, was discussed in the Columbia v. Peru case as discussed hereunder.

---

8. See dissenting opinion Judge Alvarez, International Court of Justice, Asylum Case, Colombia v. Peru, Judgment of 20.11.1950, p 30
9. Report of the Secretary-General prepared pursuant to operative paragraph 2 of the General Assembly Resolution 3321 (XXIX)

4.3 The Columbia v. Peru Case

The above-mentioned case arose around Mr. Victor Raul Haya de la Torre, who sought diplomatic asylum in the Embassy of the Republic of Columbia in Lima after he alongside others had initiated a revolution that was immediately squashed by the government of the Republic of Peru which initiated legal proceedings against Mr. de la Torre even as he was under the protection of the Columbian Embassy in Lima.

The case was brought before the International Court of Justice upon disagreement, as the Colombian government submitted that:

That the Republic of Colombia, as the country granting asylum, is competent to qualify the offense for the purpose of the said asylum, within the limits of the obligations resulting in particular from the Bolivarian Agreement on Extradition of July 18th, 1911, and the Convention on the asylum of February 20th, 1928, and of American international law in general.[10]

In their counter-memorial, the government of Peru submitted that:

As a counter-claim, under Article 63 of the Rules of Court and in the same decision, that the grant of asylum by the Colombian Ambassador at Lima to Victor Raul Haya de la Torre was made in violation of Article 1, paragraph 1, and of Article 2, paragraph 2, item I *(inciso*

10. See International Court of Justice, Asylum Case, Colombia v. Peru, Judgment of 20.11.1950, p 11

primero), of the Convention on Asylum signed in 1928, and that in any case, the maintenance of the asylum constitutes at present a violation of that treaty.[11]

In its decision, the Court would find that Colombia, as the State granting asylum, is not competent to qualify the offense by a unilateral and definitive decision, binding on Peru.[12]

However, Judge Alvarez dissented from this view, stating that according to State practice in Latin America, asylum is granted in accordance with the laws and usages of the State of refuge, and it is for the latter to appreciate whether the offense committed by the refugee is a political offense or a common crime.[13] Judge Alvarez further stresses that: "it must be pointed out that it is the State from which the asylum is requested that must decide whether it wishes to grant it or not."[14] Further, He would state that the qualification of the offense pertains to the country granting asylum, but that such qualification is not definitive, as the territorial State may contest it.[15]

Interestingly on the same day on which the Judgment was delivered, the Government of Colombia transmitted to the Registry of the Court a letter in which, its agent informed the Court that the Colombian Government wished to obtain an interpretation of the judgment of 20.11.1950 in its application, Colombia sought a reply to

11. Idem p 9
12. Idem p 16
13. See dissenting opinion Judge Alvarez, International Court of Justice, Asylum Case, Colombia v. Peru, Judgment of 20.11.1950, p 33
14. Idem p 35
15. Idem p 38

the question of whether the Judgment implied an obligation to surrender the refugee to the Peruvian authorities, to which in a Judgment delivered on 27 November 1950, the Court declared the request inadmissible.[16]

The question that arises is to identify the position of international law vis-à-vis diplomatic asylum, for instance, while several conventions regulate asylum in Latin America, for the rest of the world, where the concept of diplomatic asylum has not been codified, how is it to apply?

One needs to appreciate, on the one hand, the existence of cases of diplomatic asylum within States which have not ratified any international treaty concerning such an asylum, hence pointing at the possibility of the existence of a non-written norm governing such institution. On the other there is a certain uncertainty as to its content and contours, and how cases of abuse are handled.

Nevertheless, there is a consensus that whenever an individual is sought for political crimes, they qualify to be granted diplomatic asylum if there is any legation willing to grant them such asylum. It is at this juncture that it becomes relevant to discuss the concept of political crimes.

4.4 Political Crimes

Initially, political crimes included attempts against the life

16. See International Court of Justice, Request for interpretation of the judgment of November 20th, 1950 in the asylum case, Colombia v. Peru, judgment of 27.11.1950, p 13

of a monarch or even contemptuous behavior toward the monarch. In the wave of the French Revolution and its aftermath, in response to the support of liberal democratic revolutions and revolutionaries,[17] It was unthinkable to treat leaders of liberation movements in Europe as criminals.

Sometime between 1269 and 1284, the Egyptian Pharaoh Ramses II and the Hittite King Hattusilis III reportedly made a treaty providing for extradition.[18] Accordingly, these two entities agreed to extradite each other's enemies whenever they are found in their respective territories. A practice that remained in place for a long time.

Indeed, it is in 1833 that Belgium[19] became the first State to enact a law on the non-extradition of political offenders.[20] It was followed by France, which developed the political offense exception to shield individuals from criminal liability who may have committed acts without the "*mens rea*" required by criminal law.[21] As said by Professor Geoff Gilbert: "[T]he revolutionaries attempting to over-

17. Ronald C. Slye, "The Legitimacy of Amnesties under International Law and General Principles of Anglo-American Law: Is a Legitimate Amnesty Possible?" In Virginia Journal of International Law, Vol. 43, No. 1, 2002, p 224.
18. Ivor Stanbrook and Clive Stanbrook, Extradition: law and practice, 2nd Edition, Oxford University Press, Oxford 2000, p 3
19. M. Cherif Bassiouni, International Extradition and World Public Order, A.W. Sijthoff-Leyden, Oceana Publications Inc. - DOBBS FERRY, N.Y. 1974
20. M. Cherif Bassiouni, "Political offense exception in extradition law and practice," M. Cherif Bassiouni (Ed.) in International Terrorism and Political Crimes, Thomas Publisher, 1975, p 398.
21. Id.,

throw autocratic European regimes were the first to be protected by the political offense exemption."[22]

Today, every extradition agreement has an exception for political offenses, though they fail to define the type of offenses that fall within that concept.[23] This section provides a brief overview of different approaches towards defining "political crimes," as it analyzes the required test applicable for a better qualification of a political offense.

Finding a precise legal definition of political offense has proved impossible.[24] As said by Lord Radcliffe, in the Schtraks case, finding a definition with a sufficiently narrow scope was virtually impossible.[25] Meanwhile, Professor Cherif Bassiouni called a political offense a descriptive label of doubtful legal accuracy,[26]While M. R. Rwelamira states that not only can no one claim to have a precise definition of a political offense, it is probably as well that no such definition exists.[27] However, over time, a set of criteria has been established when dealing with the

---

22. Geoff Gilbert, Transnational Fugitive Offenders in International Law Extradition and Other Mechanisms, International Studies in Human Rights Vol. 55, Martinus Nijhoff Publishers,1998, p 247
23. Michael Forde, The Law of Extradition in the United Kingdom, The Round Hall Press, 1995, p 118.
24. Ivor Stanbrook and Clive Stanbrook, Extradition: Law and practice, 2nd Edition, Oxford University Press, 2000, p 68
25. Schtraks v Government of Israel (1964) AC 556 at 589
26. M Cherif Bassiouni, International Extradition and World Public Order, Sijthoff-Leiden, Oceana Publication, 1974
27. M R Rwelamira and G Werle, "Punishing past human rights violations: Considerations in the South African context," in Medard R. Rwelamira (Ed.) Confronting Past injustices Approaches to amnesty, punishment, reparation and restitution in South Africa and Germany, Butterworths, 1996, p 15.

political offense exception, for instance, as regards its qualification, and where applicable, its classification.

Some offenses are purely political, while others are considered to be related to political offenses. An offense is purely political when conducted directly against the sovereign or a political subdivision without causing injury to private persons, property, or interests, and without being accompanied by or having any of the elements of a common crime.[28] Offenses such as treason, sedition,[29] hostile propaganda,[30] sabotage and subversion,[31] conspiracy to overthrow the government and espionage[32] are all considered to be political offenses.

Switzerland has the narrowest definition of a political offense. Under Article 10 of the federal law on extradition to foreign states of 22 January 1892, a political offense is limited only to purely political offenses. Indeed, in its second paragraph, it states clearly that extradition will not be accorded even if the convict alleges any polit-

---

28. Christine Van den Wijngaert, The Political Offense Exception To Extradition The Delicate Problem Of Balancing The Right of Individual And The International Public Order, Kluwer-Deventer, 1980, pp 27-28

29. Michael Forde, The law of extradition in the United Kingdom, The Round Hall Press 1995, p 148

30. I.A. Shearer, Extradition in International Law, Manchester University Press, Oceana Publications Inc, 1971, p 182.

31. Ivor Stabrook and Clive Stabrook, Supra, note 267, p 69.

32. Manuel R. Garcia-Mora, Treason, Sedition and Espionage as Political Offenses under the Law of Extradition, 26 U. PITT. L. Rev. 65 1964, cited by R. Stuart Phillips, "The Political Offenses Exception and Terrorism: Its place in the Current Extradition Scheme and Proposals for its future," in Dickinson Journal of International Law, The Dickinson School of Law Vol. 15, No. 1, 1996, p 342.

ical reason[33] if the act constitutes a common crime.[34] Poncet and Neyroud have assimilated into these categories even purely military crimes[35] found exclusively under the Military Code.

4.5 Related Political Offenses

A related political offense, on the other hand, is a common crime committed for the purpose of achieving a political objective. F. Sewell has given a good illustration of the murder of a diplomat in two different scenarios; the circumstances surrounding each commission change its qualification. In the first scenario, the perpetrator and his victim are both diplomats who exchanged nationalistic insults stemming from a disagreement on an international trade protocol before the murder was committed. In the second scenario, the offender and the victim were both diplomats, but the murder occurred in the course of an argument regarding an "*affaire du coeur.*"[36] Whereas the former scenario will be easily qualified as a political offense, the latter cannot.

As said by Van den Wijngaert, related political crimes are

33. Article 10 §2 loi fédérale sur l'extradition aux États étrangers (Du 22 janvier 1892) says : « Elle [l'extradition] sera accordée, alors même que le coupable alléguerait un motif ou un but politique, si le fait pour lequel elle est demandée constitue principalement un délit commun. …. »
34. See Dominique Poncet and Philippe Neyroud, L'Extradition et l'Asile Politique en Suisse, Barblan & Saladin, Librairie de Droit, 1976, p. 75.
35. Id., p 39.
36. Alan F. Sewell, Political Crime: a Psychologist's Perspective, in M. Cherif Bassiouni, International Terrorism and Political Crimes, Thomas Publisher, 1975, p 15.

common crimes that are assimilated to political crimes because the perpetrator pursued a political purpose (subjective criterion) or the act had a political consequence (objective criterion).[37] However, in the civil law system, the motive may not necessarily be considered part of the crime, which is constituted only by its *dolus*, measured by the fact that the actor knowingly and voluntarily committed a criminal act rather than the alternative purpose at which the conduct was aimed.[38]

The only required element is the efficiency of his or her stratagems that proves the *intention doleuse*, the *animus nincendi*. As such, the *mens rea* does not take into consideration the reason, the ulterior purpose, or the motivating factor that brought about this state of mind. Instead, the criminality of an act is determined by what the perpetrator did, knew, and wanted, not the intended purpose behind the act.[39] Nevertheless, some indicators could give a useful idea upon which arguments on the qualification could be based, as below developed.

If related political crimes are common crimes to which the final motive or the circumstances in which they occur affect their qualification, the hardest task becomes determining the political motive, which may politicize a crime.

---

37. Christine Van den Wijngaert, The Political Offense Exception To Extradition The Delicate Problem Of Balancing The Right of the Individual And The International Public Order, Kluwer-Deventer, 1980, p 27
38. M. Cheriff Bassiouni, International Extradition: United States Law and Practice, Fourth Edition, Oceana Publication, Inc., Dobbs Ferry, 2002, p 608.
39. Id.,

This exercise requires the application of the predominance test.

As earlier said, pure political offenses are crimes against the State, mainly defined as such by law that do not constitute common crimes and are perpetrated without harming civilians or their property. These are clearly defined and need no additional clarification. The predominance test, therefore, applies only to related political offenses.

Two general tests determine whether an offense qualifies for the "political offense" exception. The first is the objective context approach, which focuses on the context in which the act was committed, taking into consideration questions like whether it was committed during a political uprising or conflict. The second approach is the subjective motive approach, which focuses on the motivation of the actor, taking into consideration any act committed with a political conviction. When there is a mixture of objective and subjective approaches, the crime is an incidental political crime.

Such test approaches are important in determining the application of the political crimes exception to extradition in cases with complicated fact patterns. The most eloquent example of this is the Castioni Case, in which several citizens of one of the cantons of the Swiss Republic rose against the government. They arrested several members of the government, seized the arsenal from which they provided themselves with arms, attacked, broke open, and took forcible possession of the municipal palace, disarmed the gendarmes, imprisoned members of the government, and established a provisional government. Castioni, who had taken an active part in the disturbance throughout, shot and killed a member of the government upon entering a municipal palace. He escaped to England but was arrested and was to be extradited for murder, as a common crime.

Castioni was charged with the murder of Luigi Rossi, who was a member of the State Council of the Swiss canton of Ticino, in which the revolt occurred. The extradition treaty between Switzerland and the United Kingdom included the political offense exception. In 1891, Castioni's appeal for a writ of habeas corpus came before the High Court, which unanimously allowed his appeal and released Castioni.[40] Although *habeas corpus* is defined differently in the civil and common law systems, the case gives an example of the political intent and how it can politicize a crime. In fact, the incidence test looks at the relationship between the act in question and an ongoing conflict, which is a requirement for this qualification.

The subjective approach requires a close analysis of the perpetrator's intent, which is constituted by the final aim, the motive that determined the actor. The objective approach looks at the general context in which the crime occurred and the political implications that the crime had or could have, determining whether this gives a political character to a common crime. A mixture of the two elements qualified as an incidental political crime.

---

40. See Divisional Court In Re Castioni. [1891] 1 Q.B. 149

It can thus be concluded that whenever the Head of a foreign diplomatic mission assesses that a given individual has committed a political crime, they are permitted to grant them diplomatic asylum; however, such a qualification is not binding upon the receiving State, which can always challenge it. Nevertheless, even if the receiving State does not agree with the qualification of the foreign mission, it is still under duty not to violate the immunity of such mission a situation which might leads to the concerned individual staying in the mission for an extended period of time something which could have been avoided by the territorial State granting a safe-conduit for the concerned person thus requesting that they leave their territory.

CHAPTER 5

GOVERNMENT IN EXILE

Although the phenomenon of government in exile and its recognition has been in practice for a relatively long period, there remain unanswered questions as far as the concept is concerned. Indeed while addressing the parliament of the United Kingdom on 20.02.1941, during the second reading of the Diplomatic Privileges (Extension) Bill of 1941, Mr Butler the Under-Secretary for Foreign Affairs indicated that at that time London was considered a miniature Europe as it hosted around a dozen of foreign governments in exile as a result of the occupation of their respective territories by German forces during the WWII.

Indeed, the Diplomatic Privileges (Extension) Bill was passed and became part of the laws of the United Kingdom. In its section 1(1), it stipulates that a member of the government of any foreign Power or of a provisional government being a government for the time being allied with His Majesty and established in the United Kingdom shall be treated as if they were an envoy, and his official staff shall be treated as if they were his retinue. Thus, the Act extended immunities and privileges to several governments in exile in London.

In its section 1(2), the Act created an obligation to the Secretary of State to compile and keep up-to-date a list of persons to whom immunities and privileges were extended under this law.[1] A better understanding of the concept would require a discussion on the definition of the concept of government in exile, their recognition, and the legal consequences of such recognition.

5.1 Definition

According to the Max-Planck Encyclopedia of Public International Law:

[A] government in exile consists of an individual or a group of individuals who reside within the territory of a foreign State after being forced to leave their homeland due to enemy occupation or possibly civil war. As a result, a government in exile lacks effective control over the territory of its State. Yet it claims to represent the will of the people of its homeland and, with the consent of the State of residence, asserts and possibly exercises governmental powers. The final goal of a government in exile is to (re)gain political power in its homeland.[2]

However, questions have been raised by various scholars concerning this concept. For instance, within the context of WWII, most of the governments went into exile in the United Kingdom.

After having been defeated by a foreign power, which had occupied their territories. The question then becomes

1. Stefan Talmon, recognition of the government in international law with particular reference to the government in exile, Oxford monographs in international law, 1998, p 265
2. Katrin Tiroch, Governments in Exile, Max Planck Encyclopaedia of Public International Law, 2011 para 2

whether a government in exile can emerge from a civil war situation.[3]

5.2 The Cause of the Exile

From the WWI & II cases, one might be tempted to conclude that the concept of governments in exile is only applicable to governments that have been ousted following an international armed conflict, that is to say when the said government in exile is fighting against a foreign occupation to which case one would add colonial, racist and apartheid regimes as provided for under Article 1(4) of the additional protocol I of the Geneva Convention according to which armed conflicts in which peoples are fighting against colonial domination, alien occupation or racist regimes are to be considered international conflicts.

However, State practice is not uniform, as there are governments in exile that resulted from civil wars and were recognized as such. For instance, during the Spanish Civil War of 1936- 1939, which opposed the traditional, Catholic, conservative, and liberal, leftist, democratic, republican, causing an internal armed conflict,[4] At the end of which the government was defeated and had to seek asylum in Europe and in South America, where the government was received as a Government in exile.

---

3. Katrin Tiroch, Governments in Exile, Max Planck, Encyclopedia of Public International Law, 2011, para. 3
4. Wojciech Opioła, Polish discourses concerning the Spanish Civil War. Analysis of the Polish Press 1936-2015, Central European Journal of Communication, 2017, p 211

In Africa, whereas the Empire of Haile Selassie in Ethiopia was recognized as a classic example of a government in exile by the British authorities following a military defeat by the Italians, in Sierra Leone, the exiled government was recognized by neighboring States after it had been overthrown by the regular army. Indeed, on 25 May 1997, the government of President Ahmed Tejan Kabbah, who had been elected president in March 1996 in Sierra Leone, was overthrown by a group of soldiers from the Sierra Leone Army (SLA). After the coup, which was widely condemned, President Kabbah and his government fled into exile in neighboring Guinea where it was recognized as a government in exile and benefited from all privileges and immunities thus was able to reorganize diplomatically and militarily and eventually with the support of ECOWAS, Economic Community of West African States, in March 1998, President Kabbah was reinstated as president.[5]

In a similar case, in Haiti, President Jean-Bertran Aristide, a Catholic priest, was democratically elected president on 16.12.1990; however, he was overthrown on 30.09.1991.[6] The coup drew regional and international condemnation, and President Aristide was given asylum in the USA, from where he reorganized and was able to return to Haiti. Indeed, in September 1994, after a U.S. military intervention had been launched, the military regime agreed to Aristide's return and the resignation of

5. See Human Rights Watch Country Report on Sierra Leone available at https://www.hrw.org/reports/1999/sierra/SIERLE99-02.htm
6. CRS Report for Congress, Haiti: Efforts to Restore President Aristide,1991-1994, 95-602 F, May 11, 1995

its leadership. President Aristide returned to Haiti in October 1994 under the protection of the U.S. Army.[7]

A different scenario arises from secessionist movements that are not yet formal governments and which are not fighting against any foreign power. As has been the case with previous situations, groups that are fighting for self-determination have been recognized by some States, whereas others have not. A common denominator has been that such recognition is purely a political act and has not gained uniform practice as far as States are concerned.

5.3 Competences of Governments in Exile

In the case State of the Netherlands v. Federal Reserve Bank 201F 2d 455 (2d Cir. 1953), as the Netherlands became occupied by the German conquerors, as earlier indicated, the Kingdom of the Netherlands, like many other European governments, established a Government in Exile, which promulgated a royal decree of which Article 1 provided that:

Title to claims against persons, partnerships, companies, corporations, firms, institutions, and public bodies, which claims belong to natural or legal persons domiciled in the Kingdom of the Netherlands, … in so far as these claims are in any form whatsoever capable of being encum-

7. CRS Report for Congress, Haiti: Developments and U.S. Policy Since 1991 and Current Congressional Concerns, RL32294, January 25, 2008

bered, pledged, transferred or sold or the like, outside of the Realm in Europe, is hereby vested in the State of the Netherlands, as represented by the Royal Netherlands Government, temporarily resident in London and exercising its functions there…

The same Article, in its paragraph 3, would provide that:

The proprietary rights vested in the Kingdom of the Netherlands, by virtue of the provisions of the preceding paragraphs, shall only be exercised for the conservation of the rights of the former owners.[8]

However, after occupying the Netherlands, the Germans confiscated four bonds of Dutch nationals and sold them illegally. An American citizen would acquire such bonds from a Swiss firm. The bonds were later placed in a blocked account in the Federal Reserve Bank.[9] As the plaintiff sued for the bonds, an appeal from a judgment for the defendant was reversed.[10] Indeed, the Court held that since the royal decree is not in conflict with any legitimate authority by the occupying power and does not conflict with American public policy, it must be given effect, and the Kingdom of the Netherlands was, in the end, recognized as the owner of the bonds.[11]

The President of the US had indeed signed an Executive

8. See Royal Decree A-1-CCH War Law Serv. (Foreign Supp.) 91, 251, 1940
9. John C. Hall S.Ed, International Law, power of government-in-exile to enact valid legislation, Michigan Law Review, Vol 52 Issue 5, 1954, p 753
10. See Extraterritorial enforcement of government in exile, Columbia Law Review, Volume 5, No 4, 1953, p 561
11. Idem

Order Pursuant to § 5(b) of the Trading with the Enemy Act of 1917, 12 U.S.C.A. § 95a, according to which:

All of the following transactions are prohibited, except as specifically authorized by the Secretary of the Treasury using regulations, rulings, instructions, licenses, or otherwise, if [...] such transactions involve property in which any foreign country designated in this Order, or any national thereof, has at any time on or since the effective date of this Order had any interest of any nature whatsoever, direct or indirect.[12]

The Order further states that all transfers, withdrawals, or exportations of, or dealings in, any evidence of indebtedness or evidence of ownership of property by any person within the United States; and any transaction for the purpose or which has the effect of evading or avoiding the foregoing prohibitions.[13]

As the Netherlands was recognized as one of the countries designated by the Executive order, the purchase of the bonds, which was not licensed by the Treasury, is in contravention of the Executive Order; nevertheless, the American authorities recognized the validity of the royal decree, which was issued by the government in exile.

It could be pointed out that many governments in exile might have similarities, but it remains a fact that each situation has its particularities. For instance, whereas Article 21 of the Netherlands Constitution stipulated that: "In no circumstances can the seat of the government be

12. Executive Order No. 8389, 5 Fed.Reg. 1400, of April 10, 1940
13. Idem

moved outside the realm of the Kingdom." The circumstances of WWII seem to have given grounds for the States to overlook the Constitutional provisions of the Netherlands.

However, the situation of the Polish Government in exile was different. Indeed, the Polish constitution of 1935 had made the President of the Republic a supreme organ of the State and supreme commander of armed forces, and he could extend his term as he could appoint his successor. When President Ignacy Mosciski crossed the Polish-Romanian border, the Romanian government interned the Polish government and its President.

It is under these circumstances that President Mosciski appointed Wladyslaw Raczkiewicz, who at the time had escaped and was in Paris, as his successor, who later appointed General Wladyslaw Sikorski as his Prime Minister and further appointed his cabinet, thus becoming the successor government of the pre-war government.[14] Thus answering the question asked by Samil Anatole and Max Meyer, whether the recognition of a government in exile can be extended to a newly created government without territory and continuity![15]

When it comes to the activities of the Polish government in exile, several types can be identified, primarily aid, information, and propaganda, as well as legal activities

14. See Dariusz Stola, The Polish Government-in-exile unity, and weakness, Holocaust Studies, A journal of culture and history, vol 18 No 2-3, 2012, p. 99
15. Samil Anatole Lourie and Aun Max Meyer, Government in exile and the effect of their expropriation decrees,

such as obtaining the necessary documentation needed for the identification of Polish refugees and their travel. A study of the list of documents adopted by the Polish government in exile has listed up to 554 different documents from 1939 to 1945.[16]

16. List of Documents adopted by the GiE.

CHAPTER 6

JURISDICTIONAL IMMUNITIES OF STATES AND THEIR PROPERTIES

According to Article 5 of the 2004 Convention on the jurisdictional immunity of States, a State enjoys immunity, in respect of itself and its property, from the jurisdiction of the courts of any other State. As indicated in the preamble, such a norm, which is the backbone of the 2004 Convention, is confirmed as part of international customary law.[1] The same was confirmed by the International Court of Justice in the case concerning jurisdictional immunities of the State, Germany v. Italy, as will be later discussed.

Indeed, the preamble of the 2004 Convention says that it aims at enhancing the rule of law and legal certainty, particularly in dealings of States with natural or juridical persons, as it contributes to the codification and development of international law and the harmonization of practice in this area.

As indicated by Gerhard Hafner, the 2004 Convention has solidified various norms which were scattered in various conventions but particularly the 1972 European Convention on State Immunity, the 1926 Brussels

1. The Preamble of the Convention indicates that the jurisdictional immunities of States and their property are generally accepted as a principle of customary international law

International Convention for the Unification of Certain Rules relating to the Immunity of State-owned Vessels, and others including but not limited to the 1929 Convention for the Unification of Certain Rules Relating to International Carriage by Air and the 1982 United Nations Convention on the Law of the Sea.[2]

6.1 The principle

The principle of immunity of States derives from the principle of State Sovereignty. As provided for by Article 2(1) of the UN Charter, the organization is based on the principle of the sovereign equality of all its member States. State immunity is grounded on the principle that all sovereign States are equal and independent from each other; subsequently, the principle "*par in parem non habet imperium*" applies equally to all States, that is to say that "equals do not have authority over one another."

Thus, the principle of immunity of States and their properties not only prevents courts of a foreign State from establishing jurisdiction over another State or its property, but it also bars the execution of a judgment against that State and its properties.[3] This is understood from the reading of Article 6(2), according to which:

A proceeding before a court of a State shall be considered

2. Gerhard Hafner, United Nations Convention on Jurisdictional Immunities of States and Their Property, Max-Planck Encyclopedia of International Law, 2004, para 2
3. Ferdinand Mesch, Jurisdictional Immunities of Foreign States, DePaul Law Review, Vol 23 Issue 3, 1974, p 1225

to have been instituted against another State if that other State:

a. is named as a party to that proceeding; or
b. is not named as a party to the proceeding, but the proceeding in effect seeks to affect the property, rights, interests, or activities of that other State.

Subsequently, as said by Professor Tomuschat, no member of the international community is authorized to sit in judgment over another sovereign member.[4] Indeed, Article 6(1) of the 2004 Convention stipulates that:

A State shall give effect to State immunity under Article 5 by refraining from exercising jurisdiction in a proceeding before its courts against another State, and to that end shall ensure that its courts determine on their initiative that the immunity of that other State under Article 5 is respected.

6.2 The Exception

The principle of immunity of States suffers its limitations. In general terms, a distinction is made between acts performed by a State in the exercise of its sovereign powers, known as *acta jure imperii*, for which the doctrine of States immunities applies, and acts performed by a State for private or commercial purposes, acts which are

4. Christian Tomuschat, The International Law of State Immunity and Its Development by National Institutions, Vanderbilt Journal of Transnational Law, Vol. 44, Issue 4, 2011, p 1117

known as *acta jure gestionis,* for which States immunities might not apply.[5]

For instance, chapter 97 of the US jurisdictional immunities of foreign States in its Section 1605 (a)(2) indicates that a foreign State shall not be immune from the jurisdiction of courts of the United States in any case:

[I]n which the action is based upon a commercial activity carried on in the United States by the foreign State; or upon an act performed in the United States in connection with a commercial activity of the foreign State elsewhere; or upon an act outside the territory of the United States in connection with a commercial activity of the foreign State elsewhere and that act causes a direct effect in the United States.

Switzerland, which is notable, albeit without having a statute concerning State immunity, has been able to adjudicate the matter frequently. As indicated by De Smedt, the position of Switzerland may be ascertained from its case law.[6] Indeed, the Swiss jurisprudence has developed a further criterion that must be complied with when dealing with State immunity in matters related to *acta jure gestionis*, that is, where the legal relationship giving rise to the matter should have a sufficiently close nexus to Switzerland.[7]

---

5. Vessela Terzieva, State Immunity and Victims' Rights to Access to Court, Reparation, and the Truth, International Criminal Law Review, 2022
6. Philippe De Smedt, Sovereign immunity in Switzerland and Germany, Int'l Fin. L. Rev., Vol. 20, 1983, p 20
7. Urs Feller and Marcel Frey, Switzerland: Sovereign Immunity, 2017, available on https://www.mondaq.com/sovereign-immunity-public-sec

In the matter Banque Bruxelles Lambert (Suisse) SA et huit consorts contre République du Paraguay et Sezione speciale per l'assicurazione del credito all'esportazione (recours en réforme). The Court held that, in a case in which the question of State jurisdiction immunity needed to be addressed. A distinction between acts committed as *acta jure gestionis* and *acta jure imperii* must be made. After having established that the Republic of Paraguay, by giving guarantees similar to those of a banking institution, the State acted as *jure gestionis*, the Court dismissed the motion raised by Paraguay concerning its immunity.

The facts of the case were as follows. There were various industrial projects that were being developed in Paraguay, for which two Italian companies entered into agreements with two Paraguayan companies to construct factories in Paraguay. The funds for such constructions, including the purchase of furniture and equipment, were subject to a loan given by several banks based in Geneva, with the agreement that Paraguay was the guarantor for the loans.

Indeed, Mr Gustavo Gramont Berres, Paraguayan Consul in Geneva, in the name of the Republic of Paraguay, offered two guarantees to the lending Banks. Further, the parties agreed that in case of dispute, the matter will be settled before Switzerland's judicial authorities.[8]

As it became obvious that the Paraguayan companies were unable to pay and the Republic of Paraguay failed

---

tor-government/613200/sovereign-immunity--switzerland, last consulted on 04.08.2023

8. See BGE 124 III 382 S. 384

to pay for the loan, the matter was brought before the Tribunal of First Instance, which, in its judgment of 19.12.1996, dismissed the motion raised by Paraguay concerning her State immunity. As the matter went on Appeal, on the 14. 11. In 1997, the Court of Justice of the Canton of Geneva confirmed the judgment of the Tribunal of First Instance at least on the motion raised by Paraguay on the State immunity and the jurisdiction *ratione loci*. However, as the Court of Justice nullified the judgment on other grounds, the matter was re-tried by the Federal Tribunal.

Amongst other motions, the Federal Tribunal received a motion of the Republic of Paraguay on the State Immunity that the Tribunal addressed as follows.

Referring to its jurisprudence since 1918, the Federal Tribunal indicated that it has subscribed to a restrictive interpretation of the principle of State immunity. Thus, if a foreign State acted concerning its sovereignty, such a State could raise its immunity before Swiss courts. However, if it has acted as a holder of private rights or in its private capacity, such a State can appear in Swiss courts provided that the rapport between the parties has a nexus with the Swiss territory. "*Binnenbeziehung.*"[9]

The Federal Tribunal went further as it discussed the question of the distinction between the two acts. The tribunal thus indicated that if a given State has acted with the competence of its public authority, or whether the State acted as an equal partner with other parties with

9. See BGE 124 III 382 S. 389

which the State agreed upon as any other private party would. The Tribunal indicated that, for instance, military activities, expropriation, nationalization, or decisions taken to confiscate properties of historical or archeological value are *acta juri imperii*. However, loans of States are regulated by the monetary market between parties and are thus *acta jure gestionis*.[10]

In conclusion, it was decided that the Republic of Paraguay, as guarantor, undertook to pay the lending banks the amount owed and unpaid by the Paraguayan companies. This applies as it would apply to any commitment taken by any banking institution or any other private entity, for which immunity cannot apply. The motion for State immunity was thus dismissed.

As there seems to be a consensus on the application of immunity in cases relevant to *acta jure imperii* and *acta jure gestionis*, it seems not settled whether State Immunity can be used in cases that involve *acta jure imperii* when the State has violated international law, as the matter was discussed by the International Court of Justice in Germany v. Italy, Greece intervening.

6.3 In the Case Germany v. Italy, Greece intervening

In the above-indicated case, on 23 December 2008, Germany filed in the Registry of the International Court of Justice an application instituting proceedings against Italy in respect of a dispute originating in what Germany

10. See BGE 124 III 382 S. 390

termed as violations of obligations under international law allegedly committed by Italy through its judicial practice as Germany said that Italy has failed to respect its jurisdictional immunity which Germany enjoys under international law.[11]

In its Application, Germany made several requests, including that the Court adjudge and declare that Italy, by allowing civil claims based on violations of international humanitarian law by the German Reich during World War II to be brought against Germany, committed violations of obligations under international law.[12]

Further, Germany submitted that by taking measures of constraint against 'Villa Vigoni', German State property used for government non-commercial purposes, Italy committed violations of Germany's jurisdictional immunity and that by declaring Greek judgments enforceable in Italy, it committed a further breach of Germany's jurisdictional immunity.[13]

In its pleadings Italy did not contest the *jure imperii* nature of Germany's acts, however, Italy maintained that Germany could not be entitled to immunity in respect of the cases before the Italian courts for two reasons: first, that immunity as to *acta jure imperii* does not extend to torts or delicts occasioning death, personal injury or damage to property committed on the territory of the forum State,

11. International Court of Justice, Jurisdictional Immunities of the State (Germany v. Italy: Greece intervening, Judgment of 03.02.2012, para 1
12. Idem para 15
13. dem

and, secondly, that, irrespective of where the relevant acts took place, Germany was not entitled to immunity because those acts involved the most serious violations of rules of international law of a peremptory character for which no alternative means of redress was available.[14]

In response, Germany maintained that, insofar as Italy's behavior denies a State immunity in respect of *acta jure imperii*, as no national court has ever held that a State was not entitled to immunity in respect of acts of its armed forces, Germany was entitled to the State's immunity.[15]

The International Court of Justice decided that State practice in the form of judicial decisions supports the proposition that State immunity for *acta jure imperii* continues to extend to civil proceedings for acts occasioning death, personal injury, or damage to property committed by the armed forces and other organs of a State in the conduct of armed conflict, even if the relevant acts take place on the territory of the forum State.[16] The Court then concluded that, contrary to what had been argued by Italy in the present proceedings, the decision of the Italian courts to deny immunity to Germany cannot be justified based on the territorial tort principle.[17]

14. Idem para 61
15. Idem para 63
16. Idem para 77
17. Idem para 79

6.4 The Italian Constitutional Court's Judgment No.238/2014

For the purposes of complying with the International Court of Justice judgment of 03.02.2012, which had indicated that Italy must, by enacting appropriate legislation, or by resorting to other methods of its choosing, ensure that the decisions of its courts and those of other judicial authorities infringing the immunity which Germany enjoys under international law cease to have effect,[18] Thus, the Italian parliament adopted the law no 5/2013.

According to Article 3 of the legislation, at every stage of the proceedings, the judges, even acting *proprio motu*, must declare their lack of jurisdiction when the case pending before them is one of those cases over a third State's conduct, for which the International Court of Justice has excluded the jurisdiction of the Italian civil courts.[19]

However, the Tribunal of Florence petitioned the Italian Constitutional Court, asking if the principle of sovereign equality of States, particularly in matters of immunity, can justify the sacrifice of judicial protection of fundamental rights, in cases where judicial protection is invoked against a State which has committed international crimes, albeit in the exercise of sovereign powers.[20] In a turn of

---

18. Idem, p 60
19. Chantal Meloni, Jurisdictional Immunity of States: The Italian Constitutional Court v. the International Court of Justice? Brief notes on the Judgment no. 238 of 22 October 2014 of the Italian Constitutional Court, Zeitschrift für Internationale Strafrechtsdogmatik – www.zis-online.com last consulted on 06.08.2023, p 349
20. Para 1.2

events, the Italian Constitutional Court, on 22.10.2014, declared unconstitutional the questioned law no 05/2013.

The Constitutional Court found the legislation incompatible with the right of access to justice. The Court also held that the customary rule of State immunity for *acts jure imperii*, to the extent that it was interpreted by the International Court of Justice as covering the commission of international crimes and comparable egregious violations of human rights, has never been incorporated into the Italian legal system.[21]

As it would have been expected, several legal proceedings followed the Constitutional Court judgment, some of which ordered Germany to compensate the victims. A situation that will bring Germany and Italy to the "case depart." At the time these lines are being couched, the case is all over again pending before the International Court of Justice between the two States.

6.5 The "Comfort Women" Case

In a verdict issued by the Seoul Central District Court, in the 34th Civil Chamber, Judgment Case no.: 2016 Ga-Hap 505092 of 8.01.2021, known as a compensation for damage case. The Court ordered, amongst other things, that the Defendant, the Government of Japan, should compensate a sum of 100,000,000 KRW to each Plaintiff.[22]

---

21. Riccardo Pavoni, Simoncioni v. Germany, the American Journal of International Law, vol. 109, No. 2, 2015, p 400
22. Seoul Central District Court The 34th Civil Chamber Judgment, verdict of 8.01.2021, p. 1

The facts of the case could be summarized as follows: during the military occupation of East Asia by Japan (1930-1945), the Japanese authorities, through middlemen or sometimes through their officials, abducted or recruited young women with false promises of employment to be later detained as sex slaves. The young girls were brought to "comfort stations" which were operated directly under the control of the Imperial Japanese Army, where they served as "comfort women" to the Imperial Japanese armed forces.[23]

According to the facts of the case, the Imperial Japanese authorities institutionalized the sexual slavery system as a means to boost the morale of their soldiers, but also to reduce cases of complaints by local authorities over cases of rapes, and to alleviate discontentment amongst soldiers prone to deserting the war. Such a practice also enabled the leadership to have effective command over its foot soldiers. It is further alleged that the practice was systematically planned, supported, organized, and managed by the Japanese military and other governmental institutions.[24]

The plaintiffs submitted that they were abducted by Imperial Japan from the Korean peninsula, which at that time was under the colonial rule of Japan, and they were forcibly transported out of the peninsula. They were then confined in the "comfort stations" where they were

---

23. Eleonora Branca, Yet, it moves…': The Dynamic Evolution of State Immunity in the 'Comfort Women' case, EJIL talk, last consulted 7.08.2023
24. Idem, p 33

constantly subjected to various kinds of violence, including torture and multiple rapes. [25]

The plaintiffs further submitted that they were never paid proper wages or stipends throughout the process. However, “comfort women” were afforded a weekly gynecology examination, as they were administered contraceptives and could be treated in case they contracted a sexually transmissible disease to prevent them from spreading the same to soldiers.

The Court found that such acts were illegal and that they inflicted serious physical and psychological damage to the victims. Further, the Court acknowledged that such illegal acts took place in various countries, including the Republic of Korea, China, Japan, and the South Pacific Islands. Without further elaboration on the implications of such findings, the Court stated that "the applicable laws to determine the right to claim reparations for damages due to illegal activities include laws of the Republic of Korea, China, Japan, etc."[26]

As per the facts of this case, the crime of abduction was committed in Korea, from where the victims were forcefully taken. However, the so-called "comfort stations" were located in Japan, where most of the crimes were committed, although some other crimes were committed in China. The Court did not make such an important distinction, considering that the place where the crime is alleged to have been committed is one of the key aspects of the doctrine of State immunity.

---

25. Idem, p 20
26. Idem, p 32

Indeed, the Court missed the opportunity to answer two relevant questions pertaining to this case. The Court never elaborated on the question whether a State can have jurisdiction over another State for crimes committed within the territory of the defendant, albeit when the victim is a national of the State of the forum. Secondly, it is not answered whether and if so, under which conditions the State of forum would have jurisdiction over another State, for crimes committed in a third State, and in this case, how could the Korean court have jurisdiction over crimes committed against Korean citizens by Imperial Japan in the territory of China.

As it is not settled whether the sole principle of passive nationality, according to which the State of which citizens have suffered injury has jurisdiction over the matter, even when such a case involves the immunity of the State. Further State practice will perhaps shed more light on the matter.

6.6 The Changri-La Case

The Changri-La case was named after the fishing boat that was sunk off the coast near Cabo Frio, Rio de Janeiro, by a German submarine during the Second World War in 1943.[27] When the victims' relatives took the matter to court seeking compensation, the Brazilian Courts recognized Germany's State immunity for *acta jure*

27. Ahan Gadkari, The Curious Case of Changri-La and Jurisdictional Immunities hnlusr.wordpress.com/2022/08/20 last consulted on 6.08.2013

imperii, thus concluding that dismissing the case for lack of jurisdiction before Brazilian courts.

However, on 24.11.2021, the Brazilian Supreme Court would quash the decision of the lower court by a vote of 6 to 5, holding that "wrongful acts committed by foreign States in violation of human rights do not enjoy immunity from jurisdiction."[28] Indeed, the judges of the Supreme Court referred to Article 4(II) of the Constitution, according to which the international relations of the Federative Republic of Brazil are governed by the principle of prevalence of human rights.

Contrary to the International Court of Justice in Germany v Italy, the Brazilian Supreme Court held that unlawful acts committed by foreign States in violation of human rights of humans, within national territory, do not enjoy immunity from Brazilian jurisdiction.[29]

6.7 Luxembourg District Court's Judgment 2019TALCH01 / 00116

Following a judgment of 22.12.2011 rendered by a US District Court in New York, which had entered a liability against the Islamic Republic of Iran and other defendants, including Ayatollah Ali Hossein-Khamenei, President of the Republic of Iran, and other defendants. Further, the US District Court judged in favor of the

28. Lucas Carlos Lima, Aziz Tuffi Saliba, The Immunity Saga Reaches Latin America. The Changri-la Case, EFIL talk, of 2.12. 2021
29. Eduardo Cavalcanti de Mello Filho, Karla Christina Azeredo Venâncio da Costa and Others v. Federal Republic of Germany, American Journal of International Law, Volume 117, Issue 2, 2023, p 309

Plaintiffs in the aggregate amount of 394.277.884.- USD for damages which resulted from the 11.09.2001 terrorist attack.[30]

The Plaintiffs seized the District Tribunal of Luxembourg, hereinafter "the Tribunal," to obtain the exequatur for the above judgment and for the Tribunal to order that the said judgment will have effect as if it were taken by the Tribunal.

After having referred to the International Court of Justice Judgment of 03.02.2012 in Germany v. Italy, which the Tribunal agreed with, the Tribunal held that the judge of the exequatur must make an autonomous appreciation of the legal regime applicable to the immunity of jurisdiction for any particular case before them.

The Tribunal found that the judge must satisfy themselves that the American judge has correctly applied their national law, which prevents a foreign State from claiming jurisdictional immunity, and in the present case, for the exequatur, if the case falls within the hypothesis within which international customary law provides that a foreign State should not claim jurisdictional immunity.

The judge must thus decide as if they were deciding on the substantive question of the matter. The Tribunal stated that the judge of the exequatur must apply the foreign law, but cannot limit themselves to that law alone, as they must also verify the content of the customary international law as a whole, which in this case does not

30. Judgment civil 2019TALCH01 / 00116, p 12

reveal any exception applicable to this case.[31] Therefore, the Tribunal upheld the principle of immunity of States, dismissing any action against the State of Iran.

Contrary to the reasoning of the American judge, according to whom acts of terrorism constituted an exception to the application of the principle of immunity of States, the Luxembourg judge found that such an exception cannot overthrow a norm of international customary law.

6.8 The Terrorism Exception

On 13.03.2012, Canada passed an amendment to its State Immunity Act (SIA) according to which: "A foreign State that is set out on the list [...] is not immune from the jurisdiction of a court in proceedings against it for its support of terrorism on or after January 1, 1985."[32] To follow suit was the US, which on 28.09.2016 amended its chapter 97, which provides for jurisdictional immunities of foreign States. Indeed, according to section 1605B (b):

A foreign State shall not be immune from the jurisdiction of the courts of the United States in any case in which monetary damages are sought against a foreign State for physical injury to a person or property or death occurring in the United States and caused by—

31. Idem, p 37
32. Section 6(1) State Immunity Act, Codification, Loi sur l'immunité des États, R.S.C., 1985, c. S-18

1. an act of international terrorism in the United States; and
2. a tortious act or acts of the foreign State, or of any official, employee, or agent of that foreign State while acting within the scope of his or her office, employment, or agency, regardless of where the tortious act or acts of the foreign State occurred.[33]

Other than these amendments, certain courts have also issued different kinds of decisions concerning the State immunity. It is noticeable that there is a lack of uniformity, as far as State practice is concerned; a close look at such practices will inform future opinions, as discussed below.

6.9 Relevance of the Matter and Future Perspectives

It is important to note that currently, out of 19 cases pending before the International Court of Justice, more than five cases are touching directly or indirectly on the question of the State's jurisdictional immunity. This proves how relevant the question is and how it is likely to be discussed in years to come.

As for future perspectives, since the landmark Germany v. Italy decision, there have been a few cases that have been decided by national jurisdictions. Notably, the majority but not all of them have been decided against the

33. see1605B. which provides for the responsibility of foreign States for international terrorism against the United States.

jurisprudence of the International Court of Justice, which decided the case according to current international customary law.

Indeed, customary international law is not immune to change; nevertheless, as it has been demonstrated in this chapter, a number of cases have departed from International Court of Justice jurisprudence, and there are other decisions, albeit in the minority, which decided in conformity with the position of the International Court of Justice.

If a norm of customary law is understood as a norm which is formed by State practice which is constant and general, the lack of consistency which is currently observed as far as the concept of immunity of the State is concerned is likely not to be considered as a change of State practice of a magnitude that could warrant any change of a customary norm. It thus could be predicted that the *status quo*, as articulated by the International Court of Justice in Germany v. Italy, is likely to remain.

CHAPTER 7

JURISDICTIONAL IMMUNITIES OF THE UNITED NATIONS AND ITS AGENTS

Whereas the Charter of the United Nations provides for its legal personality, stating that "the organization shall enjoy in the territory of each of its Members such legal capacity as may be necessary for the exercise of its functions and the fulfillment of its purposes."[1] It is rather Article 105 which, in paragraph 1, indicates that "the Organization shall enjoy in the territory of each of its Members such privileges and immunities as are necessary for the fulfillment of its purposes."[2]

Further, in its Article 105(2), the Charter stipulates that representatives of the Members of the United Nations and officials of the Organization shall similarly enjoy such privileges and immunities as are necessary for the independent exercise of their functions in connection with the Organization. Thus, excluding the possibility of the organization's agent enjoying any personal immunity, as some senior State officers would.

In addition, on 13.02.1946, the United Nations General Assembly adopted the resolution on the Convention on the Privileges and Immunities of the United Nations, which was opened for ratification by member states and

1. See Article 104 of the Charter of the United Nations
2. See Article 105(1) of the Charter of the United Nations

entered into force on 17.09.1946. The 1946 Convention provides that privileges and immunities are granted to officials in the interests of the United Nations and not for the personal benefit of the individuals themselves.[3] This indicates that immunity is granted to the United Nations as a matter of functional necessity.

Indeed, as earlier discussed, the concept of State immunity was first said to be founded on the abandoned principle of State extraterritoriality, then it was said to be attached to the principle of sovereignty of States, before it was understood as a functional necessity.

Perhaps, the concept of jurisdictional immunity of international organizations might clarify that the concept of immunity is not necessarily linked to the principle of territoriality nor to the principle of sovereignty, as it equally applies, albeit differently, to international institutions which do not have any territory of their own as they are hosted within the territory of their member State. Neither does the concept have to be linked to the concept of sovereignty as it applies to international organizations, which do not have any population or King and thus cannot be considered as sovereign entities per se.

It should be indicated that in international law, the concept of sovereignty *stricto senso* is directly linked to the concept of people, and with the architecture of international organizations, the population of a given nation that belongs to a given international organization remains the population of their respective nations. Such

3. See Section 20 of the 1946 Convention on the privileges and immunities of the United Nations

understanding deprives international organizations of the concept of sovereignty, which is understood differently from the concept of autonomy and independence. Thus, without being sovereign, international organizations are independent of their state members as they enjoy certain autonomy from them.

Nevertheless, international law affirms the functional necessity of diplomatic immunity and privileges granted to international organizations and their agents, irrespective of the non-application of the doctrine of extraterritoriality or the doctrine of sovereignty.

Furthermore, it is important to indicate that the source of the legality of immunity of international organizations is found within treaty law. Indeed, such immunity is provided for within the treaty creating the organization and agreement concluded between the institutions and the host State. This stands in contrast with the law on State immunity, whose immunity stems from customary international law.[4]

Much of that, one might be tempted to submit that the question of functional immunity of international organizations seems to be settled in international law, albeit in theory; in practice, the reality might point in a different direction, as discussed below.

4. Chanaka Wickremasingh, International Organizations or Institutions, Immunities before National Courts, Max Planck Encyclopedia of Public International Law

7.1 Manderlier v Organization des Nations Unies and État Belge Case

In the above-mentioned case, Mr. Menderlier, a Belgian citizen, was domiciled in the Democratic Republic of Congo at the time of the facts which gave rise to the case. Indeed, during the political turmoil that the country went through in the early 1960s, the Plaintiff witnessed his property looted and burnt by the United Nations troops, which were stationed in the Country for a peacekeeping mission.

The incident, which is recorded to have happened on 05.12.1961, left the Plaintiff aggrieved as he later filed a claim at a Belgian Tribunal based in Brussels. The Tribunal dismissed the case on the ground of jurisdictional immunity, which the United Nations enjoys before Belgian Courts. The Tribunal Civil de Bruxelles held that it had no jurisdiction over the United Nations in this case.

The case at hand raises several pertinent legal questions, amongst others, including the question directly related to the concept of functional immunity. Considering that the facts of the case indicate that the agents of the United Nations have acted outside the scope of their mandate. If such immunity is understood as being limited to the necessity of the organization's agent for the purposes of enabling them to discharge their duties, it would follow that any action performed outside of the mandate of the institution cannot be covered by such immunity, as it will be discussed later.[5]

5. See Pierre Schmitt, Menderlier v. Organisation des Nations Unies

7.2 Mothers of Srebrenica v. The Netherlands & the United Nations

The horrendous killings of Srebrenica, which were perpetrated against Bosnian Muslims by Bosnian Serb forces in the East Bosnian enclave of Srebrenica, are at the core of the case, which became known as the mother of Srebrenica before the Dutch Courts.

Indeed, the International Court of Justice in the case of Bosnia and Herzegovina v. Serbia and Montenegro has given thorough details of factual findings related to the Mothers of Srebrenica case.[6] In this case, the Court made a finding that it is established that massive killings in specific areas and detention camps throughout the territory of Bosnia and Herzegovina were perpetrated during the conflict.

Furthermore, the International Court of Justice found that the evidence presented shows that the victims of the killings were in large majority members of the protected group, which suggests that they may have been systematically targeted by the killings. Thus, the Court concluded that it was established that massive killings of members of the protected group occurred and that the requirements

---

and État Belge (Ministre des Affaires Étrangères), Tribunal Civil de Bruxelles, 11.05.1966, Journal des Tribunaux, 10.12.1966, N° 4553, 121

6. International Court of Justice, Case concerning the application of the Convention on the prevention and punishment of the crime of genocide (Bosnia and Herzegovina v. Serbia and Montenegro) Judgment of 26.02.2007

of the material element, as defined by Article II (a) of the Convention against genocide, were fulfilled.[7]

Explaining the background of the above-referred genocidal killings, Brockman-Hawe cites the Trial Chamber II of the ICTY in the case of Prosecutor v. Popovic, which found that:

In early July, these two United Nations protected areas [Srebrenica and Žepa], established as havens for civilians caught up in the calamity of war, were the subject of intense military assault by Bosnian Serb Forces. The United Nations protection forces in both places were disabled and rendered powerless. In Srebrenica, the terrified Bosnian Muslim population fled to the nearby town of Potočari. There, in the face of a catastrophic humanitarian situation, the women, children, and the elderly were ultimately loaded onto packed buses and transported away from their homes in Eastern Bosnia. For a large proportion of the male population, who were separated, captured, or had surrendered, a cataclysmic fate awaited them. Thousands of them were detained in horrific conditions and subsequently summarily executed.[8]

Thus, on June 4, 2007, a Non-Governmental Organization named the Association of the Mothers of Srebrenica, who lost their family members during the

---

7. Idem para 176
8. See Benjamin E. Brockman-Hawe, Questioning the UN's Immunity in the Dutch Courts: Unresolved issues in the mothers of Srebrenica litigation, Washington University Global Studies Law Review Volume 10, Issue 4
2011, p 729

Srebrenica killings, along with other individuals, filed a civil suit at the District Court of The Hague, against the Dutch government of The Netherlands and the United Nations as co-defendants. In this case, the Plaintiffs were seeking financial compensation from both co-defendants and acknowledgment of moral responsibility for the above-detailed killings, which took place in Srebrenica.[9] However, the District Court found that it was not competent to hear the action brought against the United Nations on account of its immunity, a decision which was later upheld by the Court of Appeal.

7.3 Distinguishing Immunity of the Organization from Immunity of its Agents

It is important to note that in a case where the United Nations is cited as a legal entity in its own capacity, particularly within the context of a possible application of the 1946 convention on the privileges and immunities of the United Nations, that is before the national courts of a State which has ratified the convention, several facts needs to be taken into consideration.

In its Article 1, the Convention recognizes the legal personality of the organization, stipulating that:

The United Nations shall possess a juridical personality. It shall have the capacity:

a. To contract

9. Idem, p. 730

b. To acquire and dispose of immovable and movable property
c. To institute legal proceedings[10]

Whereas Article 2 provides that the United Nations, its property, and assets wherever located and by whomsoever held, shall enjoy immunity from every form of legal process except insofar as in any particular case it has expressly waived its immunity shall extend to any particular case it has expressly waived its immunity.[11] Such privileges and immunities are granted to the organization to ensure its operational independence from national jurisdiction.[12]

Article 5 stipulates that officials of the United Nations shall be immune from legal process in respect of words spoken or written and all acts performed by them in their official capacity,[13] as it was clarified in the advisory opinion of the International Court of Justice in the Cumaraswamy case, as discussed later.[14]

10. See Article 1, section 1 of the 1946 Convention on the privileges and immunities of the United Nations

11. See Article 2, section 2 of the 1946 Convention on the Privileges and Immunities of the United Nations

12. See United Nations Privileges and Immunities for individuals serving on bodies established by these organizations:

Review of the legal regime and practice of organizations in the United Nations system, Technical paper, FCCC/TP/2007/2, 30 July 2007, para. 16

13. See Article 5 section 18(a) of the 1946 convention on the privileges and immunities of the United Nations

14. See International Court of Justice Advisory Opinion, Difference relating to immunity from legal process of a special rapporteur on the commission on human rights, 29.04.1999

For instance, according to section 9 of the agreement on privileges and immunities of the United Nations, concluded between the Swiss Federal Council and the United Nations, representatives of Members of the United Nations shall, while exercising their functions, enjoy the privileges and immunities. Its section 9(a) provides that:

Immunity from personal arrest or detention and seizure of their personal baggage, and, in respect of words spoken or written and all acts done by them in their capacity as representatives, immunity from legal process of every kind. [15]

Elsewhere, section 288(b) of chapter 7, subchapter XVIII on privileges and immunities of international organizations in the United States provides that:

Representatives of foreign governments in or to international organizations and officers and employees of such organizations shall be immune from suit and legal process relating to acts performed by them in their official capacity and falling within their functions as such representatives, officers, or employees, except insofar as such immunity may be waived by the foreign government or international organization concerned.[16]

It then follows that, when dealing with international orga-

15. Agreement on privileges and immunities of the United Nations concluded between the Swiss Federal Council and the Secretary-General of the United Nations on 19.04.1946

16. 22 USC chapter 7, subchapter XVIII: Privileges and Immunities of international organizations, §288d. Privileges, exemptions, and immunities of officers, employees, and their families; waiver

nizations, a distinction needs to be made between the immunity of the organization and the immunity enjoyed by its officials. By virtue of Article 2 of the above-cited 1946 Convention, as a legal entity, no legal proceedings can be instituted against the United Nations.

Indeed, as a matter of procedure, either when a motion is raised *in limine litis*, that is, as a preliminary objection at the beginning of the proceedings, or the judge could *act motu proprio*, that is, by their own initiative, declare the Court not having jurisdiction over the organization even before deciding on the substantive matter of the case. This goes as plain as yogurt or vanilla can be, depending on the case. However, what follows is not that clear.

Such an absolute bar does not exist when it comes to the immunity enjoyed by the organization's agent. When an objection on the immunity enjoyed by the agent of an organization is raised, the court is still expected to make a finding if the agent acted within their functional immunity, in which case the objection will be declared sustained; if not, the objection might be overruled, and the agent might be invited to stand the trial.

It needs to be stressed that even when an agent of an organization has acted outside their official mandate, it still becomes difficult to claim any liability from the United Nations, as it is covered by its absolute immunity, which ends up being profited by its agents whose actions are indirectly shielded by the fact that the organization enjoys immunity.

Perhaps, the only option left to a given plaintiff would be either to have the immunity of the agent of the organization waived by the same or to obtain a court judgment against the organization's official on their immunity and then initiate a claim for compensation against the agent in their individual capacity.

7.4 The Cumaraswamy Case

Mr Dato' Param Cumaraswamy, a Malaysian citizen, was appointed Special Rapporteur on the Independence of Judges and Lawyers by the United Nations Commission for Human Rights on *22.07.*1994. According to the facts of the case, in November 1995, the Special Rapporteur gave an interview to International Commercial Litigation, which is a British magazine.

During the interview, he commented on certain cases that had been adjudicated by Malaysian courts. Following the said interview, two companies filed a suit against the Special Rapporteur and claimed an amount of approximately 30 million USD as compensation for damages they claimed they had suffered as a result of the defamatory words spoken by the Rapporteur.[17]

Through its relevant organs, the United Nations made a determination that Mr. Cumaraswamy had been interviewed in his official capacity as Special Rapporteur of the Organization, and the United Nations requested the Malaysian authorities to advise Malaysian courts of the immunity from legal proceedings that the Special Rapporteur enjoyed.[18]

17. Idem, para 5
18. Idem. para 6

Further, on 20.01.1997, the Special Rapporteur filed an application requesting the Court to set aside and/or strike out the plaintiff's writ, on the ground that the words that were the subject of the suits had been spoken by him in the course of performing his mission for the United Nations as Special Rapporteur on the Independence of Judges and Lawyers thus covered by his immunity as such.[19]

Interestingly, on 28.06.1997 Malaysian High Court for Kuala Lumpur held that it was 'unable to hold that the Defendant is absolutely protected by the immunity he claims', amongst other reasons the Court found that the Secretary-General's note on the immunity of the defendant was merely 'an opinion' with scant probative value and no binding force upon the Court, thus dismissing the Mr. Cumaraswamy's motion.[20]

In a different turn of events, on 7. 11. In 1997, the Secretary-General advised the Prime Minister of Malaysia that a difference might have arisen between the United Nations and the Government of Malaysia, and about the possibility of resorting to the International Court of Justice pursuant to section 30 of the 1946 Convention, according to which:

All differences arising out of the interpretation or application of the present Convention shall be referred to the International Court of Justice unless, in any case, it is agreed by the parties to have recourse to another mode of settlement. If a difference arises between the United

19. Idem
20. Idem, para 8

Nations on the one hand and a Member on the other hand, a request shall be made for an advisory opinion on any legal question involved in accordance with Article 96 of the Charter and Article 65 of the Statute of the Court.

Contrary to the findings of the Malaysian High Court for Kuala Lumpur, the International Court of Justice, referring to the Secretary-General's findings, according to which:

Mr. Cumaraswamy had spoken the words quoted in the Article in International Commercial Litigation in his capacity as Special Rapporteur of the Commission, and he consequently was entitled to immunity from "every kind" of legal process.[21]

The International Court of Justice made a finding that the Court is of the opinion that the Secretary-General correctly found that Mr. Cumaraswamy, in speaking the words quoted in the Article in International Commercial Litigation magazine, was acting in the course of the performance of his mission as Special Rapporteur of the United Nations Commission. Consequently, Article VI, Section 22 (b), of the General Convention applies to him in the present case and affords Mr. Cumaraswamy immunity from legal process of every kind.[22]

21. Idem, para 52
22. Idem, para 56

7.5 Immunities and Privileges of States Representatives to International Organizations

It is since 1968 that the International Law Commission started working on the status of States representative to international organizations. However, due to the divergence of interests between various actors to date, the 1975 Vienna Convention on the Representation of States in their relations with the international organization of a universal character, which emanated from the work of the International Law Commission, has yet to enter into force.

Many factors might justify the lack of cohesion on this issue. In contrast to the common diplomatic relations amongst States, where all the States are at the same sending and receiving States thus benefiting directly from the reciprocity of rights and favors granted to each other and retaliating to one another when needed, the situation of State representative might be slightly different as the number of universal institutions are located in an unbalanced way mainly in the North, thus creating an unbalanced equation in the sense that whereas country in the North benefit from the prestige of hosting these international organization it comes with the consequence of hosting the diplomatic missions of member States accredited to such institutions.

Thus, during the negotiation of the 1975 Convention, building consensus became challenging between the North, on the one hand, which represented the minority of States but which hosted most of the universal organizations and their agencies, and the West and the global South, on the other hand, which represented the majority of States but which did not host many organizations.

The question of state representatives raises a second difficulty, which is related to the fact that not only do international organizations not have any territory or population, but international organizations are not just different from states; they are equally different from each other.[23] Whereas the host agreement is a bilateral treaty, always signed between the Institution and its host State, every party negotiates according to its own interests, and it is not uncommon for such a headquarter agreement not to mention the interests of other member States who are not party to the agreement.

For instance, the headquarters agreement between the Swiss Federal Council and the United Nations provides in a somewhat detailed manner about the privileges and immunities of state representatives. Indeed, Article IV, Section 9 stipulates that:

Representatives of Members of the United Nations on its principal and subsidiary organs and at conferences convened by the United Nations shall, while exercising their functions and during their journey to and from the place of meeting, enjoy the following privileges and immunities:

a. immunity from personal arrest or detention and

23. Fernando Lusa Bordin, Structural differences between States and international organizations, in the analogy between States and international organizations, Cambridge University Press, 2018, p 89

seizure of their personal baggage, and, in respect of words spoken or written and all acts done by them in their capacity as representatives, immunity from legal process of every kind;

b. inviolability for all papers and documents;
c. the right to use codes and to receive papers or correspondence by courier or in sealed bags;
d. exemption in respect of themselves and their spouses from immigration restrictions, alien registration, or national service obligations;
e. the same facilities in respect of currency or exchange restrictions as are accorded to representatives of foreign governments on temporary official missions;
f. the same immunities and facilities in respect of their personal baggage as are accorded to diplomatic envoys, and also;
g. such other privileges, immunities and facilities not inconsistent with the foregoing as diplomatic envoys enjoy, except that they shall have no right to claim exemption from customs duties on Articles imported (otherwise than as part of their personal baggage) or from indirect taxes or sales taxes.

The United States-United Nations headquarters agreement rather in its Article V providing for the resident representative in its section 15 (1) recognizes the resident representative as every person designated by a Member as the principal resident representative to the United Nations of such Member or as a resident representative with the rank of ambassador or minister plenipotentiary,

its second paragraph which provides for resident's staffs requires a prior agreement between the organization, the host State and the sending State.[24]

Thus, much that States representatives are accredited to the organization, which is hosted in the territory of another State, the role of the latter vis-à-vis the accrediting State is far from clear.

7.6 Permanent Mission to International Organizations

Article 1 (1) (7) of the 1975 Convention defines the expression permanent mission as a mission of permanent character, representing the State, sent by a State member of an international organization to the Organization.[25] Further, Article 5 stipulates that if the rules of the organization so permit, a Member State may establish a permanent mission for the performance of its functions as provided for by the Convention.

However, the same Article 5, after permitting the State member to establish its mission, creates an obligation on behalf of the organization to notify the host State before the establishment of such a mission. It is noticeable that the Convention does not create any point of contact between the sending State and the host State; further, the duty created on the organization is limited to notification,

24. Section 15(2) stipulates that "such resident members of their staffs as may be agreed upon between the Secretary-General, the Government of the United States, and the Government of the Member concerned."
25. Jean Salmon, Representatives of States in International Relations, Mepil, 2007, para 23

for which the host State of which role is not further provided for.

According to Article 6

The functions of the permanent mission consist, inter alia, of:

a. ensuring the representation of the sending State to the Organization;
b. maintaining liaison between the sending State and the Organization;
c. negotiating with and within the Organization;
d. ascertaining activities in the Organization and reporting thereon to the Government of the sending State;
e. ensuring the participation of the sending State in the activities of the Organization;
f. protecting the interests of the sending State in relation to the Organization;
g. promoting the realization of the purposes and principles of the Organization by cooperating with and within the Organization.

Thus, the main duty of the permanent mission to international organizations is to look after the interests of the sending State, amongst other things, by coordinating national representatives in various organs of the international organizations, including acting as a service center for national activities in international organizations where it is accredited.[26] As earlier said, the relationship

26. Sri Setianingsih Suwardi, 2004, Pengantar Hukum Organisasi Inter-

between the permanent mission and the State hosting the organization remains an indirect one, as it passes through the organization itself.

7.7 Permanent Observer to International Organizations

The question of the observer's status has been one of the most polarizing questions in international law. Whereas the 1975 Convention stipulates that such a status raises any queries when it is applied to any State which, without being a member State, is nevertheless interested in the work of the organization and therefore acquires the status of observer. Indeed, the 1975 Convention has gone as far as granting them the same rights as State parties.

As to the functions of such a mission, Article 7 of the 1975 Convention provides that:

The functions of the permanent observer mission consist, inter alia, of:

a. ensuring the representation of the sending State and safeguarding its interests in relation to the Organization and maintaining liaison with it;
b. ascertaining activities in the Organization and reporting thereon to the Government of the sending State;

---

nasional, Jakarta: Penerbit Universitas Indonesia, p.217 as cited by Gregorius Sri Nurhartanto, The functions and importance of representation of States in their relations with international organizations of a universal character, Lampung Journal of International Law, Volume 4 Number 1, July-December 2022, p 73

c. promoting cooperation with the Organization and negotiating with it.

However, the status of the national liberation movement and its representation has remained a subject of disagreement among various actors.[27] A better understanding of the discussion would require a brief exposé of the concept of the national liberation movement before its observer status is further studied, as it will be highlighted by a case study.

7.8 Status of National Liberation Movements

In international law, the definition of the concept of national liberation movement could be drawn from the first additional protocol to the four Geneva Conventions as an organization consisting of people who are fighting against colonial domination, alien occupation, or racist regimes in the pursuit of their right to self-determination.[28]

National liberation movements are not a recent phenomenon. Such movements have existed throughout history. However, in contemporary history, it is in the middle of the twentieth century that they progressively re-

27. Maya Hertig Randall, Vienna Convention on the Representation of States in their Relations with International Organizations of a Universal Character (1975), Max Planck Encyclopedia of Public International Law, para 6

28. See article 1 (4) of the Protocol Additional to the Geneva Conventions of 12 August 1949, and relating to the Protection of Victims of International Armed Conflicts (AP. I) of 8 June 1977

emerged as they began to appear on the international scene with their participation within the United Nations quarters through the work of the UN specialized agencies. Their legitimacy was strengthened by the wide support many movements received at the regional level, especially but not limited to Africa.

The former Organization of African Unity (OAU) played a vital role in the recognition of national liberation movements on the international scene. Some of its main objectives were to eradicate all forms of colonization from Africa and to defend the sovereignty, territorial integrity, and independence of African States.[29] At the time of its creation, the OAU was dedicated to the total emancipation of African territories that were still non-independent.[30]

Unsurprisingly, the question of decolonization was discussed during the first conference of independent African heads of state and governments. The conference established a coordinating committee tasked with harmonizing assistance from African States, including a Special Fund to be raised by voluntary contributions to assist African liberation movements. Thus, for the purposes of achieving its goal, the OAU interacted directly with national liberation movements, which the OAU recognized as representatives of the people in their respective territories.

Indeed, as indicated by Judge Abdulqawi Yusuf: "under the OAU Charter, the promotion of African unity, decol-

29. See Article 2 (1) of the 1963 OAU Charter
30. See Article 3 (3) of the 1963 OAU Charter

onization of dependent African territories... were no longer demands made in a resolution ... but a legally binding undertaking assumed by sovereign States."[31]

Thus, the appearance of national liberation movements on the international scene and their participation within the quarters was a progressive process. The legitimization of national liberation movements began with the participation of such movements in the work of the UN specialized agencies, as discussed below.

In 1958, the Economic and Social Council (ECOSOC) created the Economic Commission for Africa (ECA) as one of the UN's five regional commissions through its Resolution. 671 (XXV) of 29 April 1958. The ECA was given a mandate to facilitate concerted action for the economic development of Africa with a view to raising the level of economic activity and quality of life in Africa. Additionally, the ECA was intended to help maintain and strengthen the economic relations of African countries and territories, both among themselves and with countries throughout the world.

The ECA provided an avenue through which national liberation movements were able to gain increased legitimacy within the international community. Under Res. 1466 (XXIV) of 12 December 1959, ECOSOC Administering Members were invited to submit indigenous candidates to represent the non-self-governing Territories under their administration. These individuals would contribute to the work of technical organs of the

31. See Abdulqawi A. Yusuf, Pan-Africanism and International Law, Hague Academy of International Law, 2014, p 38

UN, either as members, associate members, or observers. However, Portugal refused to comply with this resolution.

On 24 July 1963, ECOSOC decided to expel Portugal from the ECA. Subsequently, paragraph 6 of Res. 671 (XXV) on the establishment of the ECA was amended in a manner that allowed the ECA to consider Non-Self-Governing Territories situated in Africa, Madagascar, and other African Islands as associate members. Subsequently, national liberation movements, which were recognized by regional organizations, were allowed to participate in all ECA meetings as the representatives of their people under the Portuguese administration, though without a vote.

A similar situation was to be dealt with by a different UN agency, the Special Committee on Decolonization. Created in November 1961 by UNGA Res. 1654 (XVI) on the situation with regard to the implementation of the declaration on the granting of independence to colonial countries and peoples, the mandate of the Special Committee on Decolonization is to use all means at its disposal within the framework of the procedures and modalities for the proper discharge of its functions.

However, certain Administering Powers, such as Portugal, refused to cooperate with the Special Committee. In response, the UNGA adopted Resolution 2878 (XXVI) on the Implementation of the Declaration on the Granting of Independence to Colonial Countries and Peoples of 20 December 1971. This resolution endorsed the proposal of the Special Committee to 'take steps in consultation with the Organization of African Unity, to enable representation of national liberation movements in the colonial Territories in Southern Africa to participate, whenever necessary and in an appropriate capacity, in its deliberations relating to those territories.' This resolution gave national liberation movements inroads into the UN institutions.

7.9 National Liberation Movement and the UNGA

Although national liberation movements were recognized as representatives of the people of their territories by the Economic Commission for Africa, which was created by the Economic and Social Council (ECOSOC), the Special Committee on Decolonization, and the OAU, they were not automatically accepted as such by the UNGA. Rather, national liberation movements began to participate in the works of the UNGA through direct petitions made by leaders of these movements in their private individual capacities. Similarly, individual participation was also given to missionaries, journalists, or any other person whose communication was considered useful during sessions of UN institutions.[32]

However, participation through petitions would prove inadequate for national liberation movements due to their limitations. Although petitions for participation were

32. See, for instance, Res 1804 (XVII) on petitions and communication related to the territory of South West Africa of 14 December 1962; Res. 1812 (XVII) on the Question of Kenya, of 17 December 1962; Res. 1817 (XVII) on the Question of Basutoland, Bechuanaland and Swaziland of 18 December 1962, etc...

often allowed, no right to petition existed within the UN procedural rules. Consequently, each UN organ had the discretion to decide whether to grant a request or not. Another limiting factor to participation through petitions is its passive nature, as representatives had no right to participate in discussions during sessions unless asked questions following their petitions. After a lengthy debate, the UNGA allowed national liberation movements, which were recognized by their respective regional organizations, to participate in its work as representatives of the people within their relevant territories and later granted them observer status.

7.10 Recognition as Observer

By 1974, recognized national liberation movements could participate in UN discussions concerning their territories as representatives of the people in their respective territories. Consequently, the UNGA decided through Res. 3210 (XXIX) to invite the Palestine Liberation Organization (PLO) of 14 October 1974 to invite the PLO to participate in its plenary meetings as the representative of the Palestinian people.

Initially, national liberation movements participated in the work of the UN special agencies solely on issues related to their territories. However, the PLO's participation was not limited to issues related to the Palestine territory because it was upgraded to the status of observer. Rather, the PLO gained the right to participate in all UNGA deliberations, though without a vote.

A similar formula was used in Res. 31/152 on the observer status for the South West Africa People's Organization (SWAPO). The resolution granted the status of observer to SWAPO, which it had earlier recognized as the authentic representative of the Namibian people.[33] The same resolution invited the movement to participate in the sessions and the work of the General Assembly.

7.11 United States v. Palestine Liberation Organization

As indicated earlier, after the United Nations recognized the Palestine Liberation Organization as a national liberation movement and granted it observer status, it was invited to participate in the sessions and the work of the United Nations General Assembly. Seizing the opportunity, the PLO decided to establish a permanent mission to the UN, a mission which was to be based in New York.

Soon after such a mission was established, a case was brought before the Court challenging the admission of the movement to the United States territory. The US Court held that:

This problem must be viewed in the context of the special responsibility that the United Nations has to provide access to the United Nations under the Headquarters Agreement. It is important to note for this case that a primary goal of the United Nations is to provide a forum

33. See Res. 3111 (XXVIII) on the Question of Namibia of 21 December 1973.

where peaceful discussions may displace violence as a means of resolving disputed issues.[34]

Thus, the movement established its permanent mission and was allowed to function within the United States of America as a permanent observer to the United Nations, as per its status according to the Headquarters agreement.

Nevertheless, following the increase in terrorist attacks against American citizens, a section of Congressmen in the US requested the State Department to close the Palestine Liberation Organization mission in retaliation for such attacks. After the failure of their initial endeavor, a bill was passed by Congress that aimed at the closure of the movement's mission.[35]

The bill resulted in the Anti-Terrorist Act and entered into force in March 1988. Pursuant to the Act, Congress made a determination stating that "Congress determines that the PLO and its affiliates are a terrorist organization and a threat to the interests of the United States, its allies, and to international law and should not benefit from operating in the United States."[36]

The same day the Act took effect, the United States

---

34. See Anti-Defamation League of B'nai B'rith v. Kissinger, Civil Action No. 74 C 1545 (E.D. N.Y. November 1, 1974), excerpted in Department of State, 1974 Digest of United States Practice in International Law, 27, 28

35. Andrew R. Horne, United States v. Palestine Liberation Organization: Continued Confusion in Congressional Intent and the Hierarchy of Norms, Michigan Journal of International Law, Vol. 10 Issue 3, 1989, p 936

36. 22 U.S.C. § 5201 Section 5201 - Findings; determinations

Attorney for the District commenced a lawsuit as he requested the Court to grant an injunctive relief for the purposes of enabling them to proceed with the closure of the mission. After having determined that:

[T]he court finds that it is not deprived of subject matter jurisdiction by Section 21 of the Headquarters Agreement and that any interpretation of the Headquarters Agreement incident to an interpretation of the ATA must be done by the court.[37]

Referring to section 11 of the Headquarters Agreement, according to which

The federal State, or local authorities of the United States, shall not impose any impediments to transit to or from the headquarters district of (1)representatives of Members ..., (5) other persons invited to the headquarters district by the United Nations ... on official business.

The Court decided that "the language, application, and interpretation of the Headquarters Agreement leads us to the conclusion that it requires the United States to refrain from interference with the PLO Observer Mission in the discharge of its functions at the United Nations."[38]

The Court reasoned that the Anti-Terrorist Act and the Headquarters Agreement cannot be reconciled except by finding the ATA inapplicable to the Palestine Liberation Organization Observer Mission. As it further found the

---

37. United States v. Palestine Liberation Organization, 695 F. Supp. 1456(S.D.N.Y. 1988), U.S. District Court for the Southern District of New York - 695 F. Supp. 1456(S.D.N.Y. 1988) June 29, 1988, p 12
38. Idem p 14

obligation of the United States to allow transit, entry, and access stems not only from the language of the Headquarters Agreement but also from forty years of practice under it. Thus, the PLO was once again allowed to continue operating from the US territory.

CONCLUDING NOTES

After having discussed the key concepts relevant to diplomatic relations between States, the research discussed the establishment of diplomatic relations and diplomatic missions through a study of the relevant legal provisions and States ' practice. It is followed by a chapter discussing immunities and privileges of the staff of foreign missions, diplomatic and non-diplomatic staff.

The research continues with a discussion on the concept of diplomatic asylum, drawing a balance between the existing doctrine and the relevant State practice as reflected in domestic legislation and decisions of various domestic courts. A discussion on the concept of government in exile, which studies the competence of such governments, the causes that lead them into exile, complemented by a discussion on various examples of such governments.

In its following chapter, the study turns to the investigation of the concept of jurisdictional immunities of States and their properties, by discussing the applicable principle, and its exceptions, before it reviews some relevant cases. A chapter connected to the previous chapter studies jurisdictional immunities of international organizations of universal character.

This chapter reviews relevant cases as decided by various courts, including international and domestic courts, as it reviews relevant legislation either at the domestic level or at the international level. The study is concluded by a challenging discussion on representation before international organizations, particularly the representation of national liberation movements, as it focuses on two examples of such movements, the SWAPO and the PLO.

Without claiming to have exhaustively dealt with the subject, this research has rather highlighted some of the controversial issues, as it is only designed to stimulate the debate amongst scholars and practitioners on various topics, and looks forward to further discussions.

SELECTED BIBLIOGRAPHY

Published Works

Aaron X. Fellmeth and Maurice Horwitz, Guide to Latin in international law, Oxford University Press, 2009

Abdulqawi A. Yusuf, Pan-Africanism and International Law, Hague Academy of International Law, 2014

Adeoye Akinsanya, The Dikko Affair and Anglo-Nigerian Relations, The International and Comparative Law Quarterly, No 3, Vol 34, 1985

Ahan Gadkari, The Curious Case of Changri-La and Jurisdictional Immunities hnlusr.wordpress.com/2022/08/20

Alan F. Sewell, Political Crime: a Psychologist's Perspective, in M. Cherif Bassiouni, International Terrorism and Political Crimes, Thomas Publisher, 1975

Alina Malinowska, The institution of diplomatic asylum as the possibility of protecting human rights, European Journal of International Law

Andrew R. Horne, United States v. Palestine Liberation Organization: Continued Confusion in Congressional Intent and the Hierarchy of Norms, Michigan Journal of International Law, Vol. 10 Issue 3, 1989

Anti-Defamation League of B'nai B'rith v. Kissinger, Civil Action No. 74 C 1545 (E.D. N.Y. November 1, 1974), excerpted in Department of State, 1974 Digest of United States Practice in International Law, 27, 28

Antony Aust, Handbook of international law, Cambridge University Press, 2005

Benjamin E. Brockman-Hawe, Questioning the UN's Immunity in the Dutch Courts: Unresolved issues in the mothers of Srebrenica litigation, Washington University Global Studies Law Review Volume 10 Issue 4

Chanaka Wickremasingh, International Organizations or Institutions, Immunities before National Courts, Mepil,

Christian Tomuschat, The International Law of State Immunity and Its

Development by National Institutions, Vanderbilt Journal of Transnational Law, Vol. 44, Issue 4, 2011

Christine M. Nelson, "Opening Pandora's Box: The Status of the Diplomatic Bag in International Relations, Fordham International Law Journal, Volume 12, Issue 3, 1988

Christine Van den Wijngaert, The Political Offense Exception To Extradition: The Delicate Problem Of Balancing The Right of the Individual And The International Public Order, Kluwer-Deventer, 1980

CRS Report for Congress, Haiti: Developments and U.S. Policy Since 1991 and Current Congressional Concerns, RL32294, January 25, 2008

CRS Report for Congress, Haiti: Efforts to Restore President Aristide,1991-1994, 95-602 F, May 11, 1995

Dariusz Stola, The Polish Government-in-exile unity, and weakness, Holocaust Studies, A journal of culture and history, vol 18 No 2-3, 2012

Dominique Poncet and Philippe Neyroud, L'Extradition et l'Asile Politique en Suisse, Barblan&Saladin, Librairie de Droit, 1976

Draft Articles on the Status of the Diplomatic Courier and the Diplomatic Bag Not Accompanied by Diplomatic Courier

Draft Optional Protocols 1989

Eduardo Cavalcanti de Mello Filho, Karla Christina Azeredo Venâncio da Costa and Others v. Federal Republic of Germany, American Journal of International Law, Volume 117, Issue 2, 2023

Egidio Reale, "Le droit d'asile," Recueil des cours de l'Académie de droit international, 1938, vol. I, p. 513, as cited by the Report of the Secretary-General prepared pursuant to operative paragraph 2 of the General Assembly Resolution 3321 (XXIX)

Eleonora Branca, Yet, it moves…': The Dynamic Evolution of State Immunity in the 'Comfort Women' case, EJIL Talk, last consulted 7.08.2023

Elizabeth A. Martin, (Ed) Oxford Dictionary of Law, 5th Edition, Oxford University Press, 2003

Ernest Satow, A guide to diplomatic practice, Vol. 1, Cambridge Library Collection, 1917

Ferdinand Mesch, Jurisdictional Immunities of Foreign States, DePaul Law Review, Vol 23 Issue 3, 1974

Fernando Lusa Bordin, Structural differences between States and international organizations, in the analogy between States and international organizations, Cambridge University Press, 2018

Geoff Gilbert, Transnational Fugitive Offenders in International Law Extradition and Other Mechanisms, International Studies in Human Rights Vol. 55, Martinus Nijhoff Publishers,1998

Gerhard Hafner, United Nations Convention on Jurisdictional Immunities of States and Their Property, Max-Planck Encyclopedia of International Law, 2004

Gracieux Mbuzukongira, Enforcement mechanism to implement international law standards for the protection of refugees: The Rwandan refugees in the DRC case, Common Ground, 2013

Grant V. McClanahan, Diplomatic immunity: Principles, practice, problems, Hurst & Co., 1976

Gregorius Sri Nurhartanto, The functions and importance of representation of States in their relations with international organizations of a universal character, Lampung Journal of International Law, Volume 4 Number 1, July-December 2022

Hersch Lauterpacht, Recognition in international law, Cambridge University Press, 1947

Holger P Hestermeyer, Vienna Convention on Diplomatic Relations (1961), Max-Planck Encyclopedia of International Law, 2009

I A. Shearer, Extradition in International Law, Manchester University Press, Oceana Publications Inc, 1971

Ivor Stanbrook and Clive Stanbrook, Extradition: Law and Practice, 2nd Edition, Oxford University Press, 2000

Jean d'Aspremont, Persona Non Grata, Max Planck Encyclopedia of Public International Law, 2009

Jean Salmon, Manuel de droit diplomatique, Bruylant Bruxelles, 1994

Jean Salmon, Representatives of States in International Relations, Max-Planck Encyclopedia of International Law, 2007

John C. Hall S.Ed, International Law, power of government-in-exile to enact valid legislation, Michigan Law Review, Vol 52, Issue 5, 1954

Katrin Tiroch, Governments in Exile, Max Planck Encyclopedia of Public International Law, 2011

Lucas Carlos Lima, Aziz Tuffi Saliba, The Immunity Saga Reaches Latin America. The Changri-la Case, EJIL talk, 2.12. 2021

M Cherif Bassiouni, International Extradition and World Public Order, Sijthoff-Leiden, Oceana Publication, 1974

M. Cherif Bassiouni (Ed.) in International Terrorism and Political Crimes, Thomas Publisher, 1975

M. Cherif Bassiouni, International Extradition and World Public Order, A.W. Sijthoff- R. Stuart Phillips, "The Political Offenses Exception and Terrorism: Its place in the Current Extradition Scheme and

Proposals for its future," in Dickinson Journal of International Law, The Dickinson School of Law Vol. 15, No. 1, 1996

Maria Aristodemou, Choice and evasion in Judicial recognition of government, 5 European Journal of International Law, 1994

Matthias Herdegen, The Abuse of Diplomatic Privileges and Countermeasures not Covered by the Vienna Convention on Diplomatic Relations, Some Observations in the Light of Recent Experience, Max-Planck-Institut für ausländisches öffentliches Recht und Völkerrecht, 1986

Maya Hertig Randall, Vienna Convention on the Representation of States in their Relations with International Organizations of a Universal Character (1975), Max-Planck Encyclopedia of International Law

Medard R. Rwelamira (Ed.) Confronting Past Injustices: Approaches to Amnesty, Punishment, Reparation and Restitution in South Africa and Germany, Butterworths, 1996

Michael Forde, The Law of Extradition in the United Kingdom, The Round Hall Press, 1995

Philippe De Smedt, Sovereign immunity in Switzerland and Germany, Int'l Fin. L. Rev., Vol. 20. 1983

Pierre Schmitt, Menderlier v. Organisation des Nations Unies and État belge (Ministre des Affaires Étrangères), Tribunal civil de Bruxelles, 11.05.1966, Journal des Tribunaux, 10.12.1966, n° 4553, 121

Ralp G. Feltham, the diplomatic mission, in Diplomatic handbook, Brill, 2004

René Värk, Personal inviolability and diplomatic immunity in respect of serious crimes, Juridica International, VIII/ 2003

Report of the Secretary-General prepared pursuant to operative paragraph 2 of the General Assembly Resolution 3321 (XXIX)

Review of the legal regime and practice of organizations in the United Nations system, Technical paper, FCCC/TP/2007/2, 30 July 2007

Riccardo Pavoni, Simoncioni v. Germany, the American Journal of International Law, vol. 109, No. 2, 2015

Ronald C. Slye, "The Legitimacy of Amnesties under International Law and General Principles of Anglo-American Law: Is a Legitimate Amnesty Possible?" In Virginia Journal of International Law, Vol. 43, No. 1, 2002

Rosanne van Alebeek, Diplomatic immunity, in Max Planck Encyclopedia of Public International Law

S. Prakash Sinha, Diplomatic Asylum, Asylum in international law, Martinus Nijhoff, 1971

Sir Arthur Watts, The legal position in international law of heads of states, heads of governments and foreign ministers, in 3 Recueil des Cours 20, 1994

Stefan Talmon, Recognition of the Government in International Law, with particular reference to the government in exile, Oxford University Press, 2001

Vessela Terzieva, State Immunity and Victims' Rights to Access to Court, Reparation, and the Truth, International Criminal Law Review, 2022

Vienna - 2 March - 14 April 1961 Official Records Volume II: Annexes Final Act Vienna Convention on Diplomatic Relations Optional Protocols Resolutions

Wojciech Opioła, Polish discourses concerning the Spanish Civil War. Analysis of the Polish Press 1936-2015, Central European Journal of Communication, 2017

Legal and Quasi-Legal Sources

1946 convention on the privileges and immunities of the United Nations

1961 Vienna Convention on Diplomatic Relations

1963 OAU Charter

1973 Vienna Convention on Consular Relations

22 U.S.C. § 5201 Section 5201 - Findings; determinations

22 USC chapter 7, subchapter XVIII: Privileges and Immunities of international organizations, §288d. Privileges, exemptions, and immunities of officers, employees, and their families; waiver

A.CONF2O/14 United Nations Conference on Diplomatic Intercourse and Immunities Vienna — 2 March - 14 April 1961 Official Records Volume I: Summary Records of Plenary Meetings and Meetings of the Committee of the Whole

A/CN.4/SR.509 Summary record of the 509th meeting, Consular intercourse and immunities. Extract from the Yearbook of the International Law Commission: 1959, vol. I

A/CONF.20/14/Add. The United Nations Conference on Diplomatic Intercourse and Immunities

A/CONF.20/C.1/L.17 United States of America: amendments to Article 1, 6 March 1961

A/CONF.20/C.1/L.90 India: amendment to Article 1, 8 March 1961

A/CONF.20/C.1/L.91, Ceylon: amendment to Article 1, 8 March 1961

Agreement on privileges and immunities of the United Nations concluded between the Swiss Federal Council and the Secretary-General of the United Nations on 19.04.1946

Charter of the United Nations

Protocol Additional to the Geneva Conventions of 12 August 1949, and relating to the Protection of Victims of International Armed Conflicts (AP. I) of 8 June 1977

Res. 3111 (XXVIII) on the Question of Namibia of 21 December 1973.

Royal Decree A-1-CCH War Law Serv. (Foreign Supp.) 91, 251, 1940

Section 6(1) State Immunity Act, Codification, Loi sur l'immunité des États, R.S.C., 1985, c. S-18

List of Cases

International Court of Justice Advisory Opinion, Difference relating to immunity from legal process of a special rapporteur on the commission on human rights, 29.04.1999

International Court of Justice, Asylum Case, Colombia v. Peru, Judgment of 20.11.1950

International Court of Justice, Case concerning Armed Activities on the territory of the Congo, (Democratic Republic of the Congo v. Uganda) Judgment of 19 December 2005

International Court of Justice, Case concerning the application of the Convention on the prevention and punishment of the crime of genocide (Bosnia and Herzegovina v. Serbia and Montenegro) Judgment of 26.02.2007

International Court of Justice, Case concerning the arrest warrant of 11 April 2000, Democratic Republic of Cong v. Belgium, Judgment of 14 February 2002

International Court of Justice, Case concerning United States Diplomats and Consular Staff in Tehran, (United States of America v. Iran), Judgment of 24 May 1980

International Court of Justice, Jurisdictional Immunities of the State (Germany v. Italy: Greece intervening, Judgment of 03.02.2012

International Court of Justice, Request for interpretation of the judgment of November 20th, 1950 in the asylum case, Colombia v. Peru, judgment of 27.11.1950

Schtraks v Government of Israel (1964) AC 556

Seoul Central District Court, The 34th Civil Chamber Judgment, verdict of 8.01.2021

United States v. Palestine Liberation Organization, 695 F. Supp.

1456(S.D.N.Y. 1988), U.S. District Court for the Southern District of New York - 695 F. Supp. 1456(S.D.N.Y. 1988) June 29, 1988

ANNEX

Vienna Convention on Diplomatic Relations 1961

Done at Vienna on 18 April 1961. Entered into force on 24 April 1964. United Nations, *Treaty Series*, vol. 500, p. 95.

Vienna Convention on Diplomatic Relations Done at Vienna on 18 April 1961

The States Parties to the present Convention,

Recalling that peoples of all nations from ancient times have recognized the status of diplomatic agents,

Having in mind the purposes and principles of the Charter of the United Nations concerning the sovereign equality of States, the maintenance of international peace and security, and the promotion of friendly relations among nations,

Believing that an international convention on diplomatic intercourse, privileges and immunities would contribute to the development of friendly relations among nations, irrespective of their differing constitutional and social systems,

Realizing that the purpose of such privileges and immunities is not to benefit individuals but to ensure the efficient performance of the functions of diplomatic missions as representing States,

Affirming that the rules of customary international law should continue to govern questions not expressly regulated by the provisions of the present Convention,

Have agreed as follows:

Article 1

For the purpose of the present Convention, the following

expressions shall have the meanings hereunder assigned to them:

a. The "head of the mission" is the person charged by the sending State with the duty of acting in that capacity;

b. The "members of the mission" are the head of the mission and the members of the staff of the mission;

c. The "members of the staff of the mission" are the members of the diplomatic staff, of the administrative and technical staff and of the service staff of the mission;

d. The "members of the diplomatic staff" are the members of the staff of the mission having diplomatic rank;

e. A "diplomatic agent" is the head of the mission or a member of the diplomatic staff of the mission;

f. The "members of the administrative and technical staff" are the members of the staff of the mission employed in the administrative and technical service of the mission;

g. The "members of the service staff" are the members of the staff of the mission in the domestic service of the mission;

h. A “private servant” is a person who is in the domestic service of a member of the mission and who is not an employee of the sending State;

i. The “premises of the mission” are the buildings or parts of buildings and the land ancillary thereto, irrespective of ownership, used for the purposes of the mission including the residence of the head of the mission.

Article 2

The establishment of diplomatic relations between States, and of permanent diplomatic missions, takes place by mutual consent.

Article 3

1. The functions of a diplomatic mission consist, inter alia, in:

a. Representing the sending State in the receiving State;

b. Protecting in the receiving State the interests of the sending State and of its nationals, within the limits permitted by international law;

c. Negotiating with the Government of the receiving State;

d. Ascertaining by all lawful means conditions and developments in the receiving State, and reporting thereon to the Government of the sending State;

e. Promoting friendly relations between the sending State and the receiving State, and developing their economic, cultural and scientific relations.

2. Nothing in the present Convention shall be construed as preventing the performance of consular functions by a diplomatic mission.

Article 4

1. The sending State must make certain that the *agrément* of the receiving State has been given for the person it proposes to accredit as head of the mission to that State.

2. The receiving State is not obliged to give reasons to the sending State for a refusal of *agrément*.

Article 5

1. The sending State may, after it has given due notification to the receiving States concerned, accredit a head of mission or assign any member of the diplomatic staff, as the case may be, to more than one State, unless there is express objection by any of the receiving States.

2. If the sending State accredits a head of mission to one or more other States it may establish a diplomatic mission

headed by a chargé d'affaires ad interim in each State where the head of mission has not his permanent seat.

3. A head of mission or any member of the diplomatic staff of the mission may act as representative of the sending State to any international organization.

Article 6

Two or more States may accredit the same person as head of mission to another State, unless objection is offered by the receiving State.

Article 7

Subject to the provisions of articles 5, 8, 9 and 11, the sending State may freely appoint the members of the staff of the mission. In the case of military, naval or air attachés, the receiving State may require their names to be submitted beforehand, for its approval.

Article 8

1. Members of the diplomatic staff of the mission should in principle be of the nationality of the sending State.

2. Members of the diplomatic staff of the mission may not be appointed from among persons having the nationality of the receiving State, except with the consent of that State which may be withdrawn at any time.

3. The receiving State may reserve the same right with

regard to nationals of a third State who are not also nationals of the sending State.

Article 9

1. The receiving State may at any time and without having to explain its decision, notify the sending State that the head of the mission or any member of the diplomatic staff of the mission is persona non grata or that any other member of the staff of the mission is not acceptable. In any such case, the sending State shall, as appropriate, either recall the person concerned or terminate his functions with the mission. A person may be declared non grata or not acceptable before arriving in the territory of the receiving State.

2. If the sending State refuses or fails within a reasonable period to carry out its obligations under paragraph 1 of this article, the receiving State may refuse to recognize the person concerned as a member of the mission.

Article 10

1. The Ministry for Foreign Affairs of the receiving State, or such other ministry as may be agreed, shall be notified of:

a. The appointment of members of the mission, their arrival and their final departure or the termination of their functions with the mission;

b. The arrival and final departure of a person belonging to the family of a member of the mission and, where appropriate, the fact that a person becomes or ceases to be a member of the family of a member of the mission;

c. The arrival and final departure of private servants in the employ of persons referred to in subparagraph (*a*) of this paragraph and, where appropriate, the fact that they are leaving the employ of such persons;

d. The engagement and discharge of persons resident in the receiving State as members of the mission or private servants entitled to privileges and immunities.

2. Where possible, prior notification of arrival and final departure shall also be given.

Article 11

1. In the absence of specific agreement as to the size of the mission, the receiving State may require that the size of a mission be kept within limits considered by it to be reasonable and normal, having regard to circumstances and conditions in the receiving State and to the needs of the particular mission.

2. The receiving State may equally, within similar bounds and on a non-discriminatory basis, refuse to accept officials of a particular category.

Article 12

The sending State may not, without the prior express consent of the receiving State, establish offices forming part of the mission in localities other than those in which the mission itself is established.

Article 13

1. The head of the mission is considered as having taken up his functions in the receiving State either when he has presented his credentials or when he has notified his arrival and a true copy of his credentials has been presented to the Ministry for Foreign Affairs of the receiving State, or such other ministry as may be agreed, in accordance with the practice prevailing in the receiving State which shall be applied in a uniform manner.

2. The order of presentation of credentials or of a true copy thereof will be determined by the date and time of the arrival of the head of the mission.

Article 14

1. Heads of mission are divided into three classes, namely:

a. That of ambassadors or nuncios accredited to Heads of State, and other heads of mission of equivalent rank;

b. That of envoys, ministers and internuncios accredited to Heads of State;

c. That of chargés d'affaires accredited to Ministers for Foreign Affairs.

2. Except as concerns precedence and etiquette, there shall be no differentiation between heads of mission by reason of their class.

Article 15

The class to which the heads of their missions are to be assigned shall be agreed between States.

Article 16

1. Heads of mission shall take precedence in their respective classes in the order of the date and time of taking up their functions in accordance with article 13.

2. Alterations in the credentials of a head of mission not involving any change of class shall not affect his precedence.

3. This article is without prejudice to any practice accepted by the receiving State regarding the precedence of the representative of the Holy See.

Article 17

The precedence of the members of the diplomatic staff of the mission shall be notified by the head of the mission to the Ministry for Foreign Affairs or such other ministry as may be agreed.

Article 18

The procedure to be observed in each State for the reception of heads of mission shall be uniform in respect of each class.

Article 19

1. If the post of head of the mission is vacant, or if the head of the mission is unable to perform his functions a chargé d'affaires ad interim shall act provisionally as head of the mission. The name of the chargé d'affaires ad interim shall be notified, either by the head of the mission or, in case he is unable to do so, by the Ministry for Foreign Affairs of the sending State to the Ministry for Foreign Affairs of the receiving State or such other ministry as may be agreed.

2. In cases where no member of the diplomatic staff of the mission is present in the receiving State, a member of the administrative and technical staff may, with the consent of the receiving State, be designated by the sending State to be in charge of the current administrative affairs of the mission.

Article 20

The mission and its head shall have the right to use the flag and emblem of the sending State on the premises of the mission, including the residence of the head of the mission, and on his means of transport.

Article 21

1. The receiving State shall either facilitate the acquisition on its territory, in accordance with its laws, by the sending State of premises necessary for its mission or assist the latter in obtaining accommodation in some other way.

2. It shall also, where necessary, assist missions in obtaining suitable accommodation for their members.

Article 22

1. The premises of the mission shall be inviolable. The agents of the receiving State may not enter them, except with the consent of the head of the mission.

2. The receiving State is under a special duty to take all appropriate steps to protect the premises of the mission against any intrusion or damage and to prevent any disturbance of the peace of the mission or impairment of its dignity.

3. The premises of the mission, their furnishings and other property thereon and the means of transport of the mission shall be immune from search, requisition, attachment or execution.

Article 23

1. The sending State and the head of the mission shall be exempt from all national, regional or municipal dues and taxes in respect of the premises of the mission, whether owned or leased, other than such as represent payment for specific services rendered.

2. The exemption from taxation referred to in this article shall not apply to such dues and taxes payable under the law of the receiving State by persons contracting with the sending State or the head of the mission.

Article 24

The archives and documents of the mission shall be inviolable at any time and wherever they may

be.

Article 25

The receiving State shall accord full facilities for the performance of the functions of the mission.

Article 26

Subject to its laws and regulations concerning zones entry into which is prohibited or regulated for reasons of national security, the receiving State shall ensure to all members of the mission freedom of movement and travel in its territory.

Article 27

1. The receiving State shall permit and protect free communication on the part of the mission for all official purposes. In communicating with the Government and the other missions and consulates of the sending State, wherever situated, the mission may employ all appropriate means, including diplomatic couriers and messages in code or cipher. However, the mission may install and use a wireless transmitter only with the consent of the receiving State.

2. The official correspondence of the mission shall be inviolable. Official correspondence means all correspondence relating to the mission and its functions.

3. The diplomatic bag shall not be opened or detained.

4. The packages constituting the diplomatic bag must bear visible external marks of their character and may contain only diplomatic documents or articles intended for official use.

5. The diplomatic courier, who shall be provided with an official document indicating his status and the number of packages constituting the diplomatic bag, shall be protected by the receiving State in the performance of his functions. He shall enjoy person inviolability and shall not be liable to any form of arrest or detention.

6. The sending State or the mission may designate diplomatic couriers ad hoc. In such cases the provisions of paragraph 5 of this article shall also apply, except that the immunities therein mentioned shall cease to apply when

such a courier has delivered to the consignee the diplomatic bag in his charge.

7. A diplomatic bag may be entrusted to the captain of a commercial aircraft scheduled to land at an authorized port of entry. He shall be provided with an official document indicating the number of packages constituting the bag but he shall not be considered to be a diplomatic courier. The mission may send one of its members to take possession of the diplomatic bag directly and freely from the captain of the aircraft.

Article 28

The fees and charges levied by the mission in the course of its official duties shall be exempt from all dues and taxes.

Article 29

The person of a diplomatic agent shall be inviolable. He shall not be liable to any form of arrest or detention. The receiving State shall treat him with due respect and shall take all appropriate steps to prevent any attack on his person, freedom or dignity.

Article 30

1. The private residence of a diplomatic agent shall enjoy the same inviolability and protection as the premises of the mission.

2. His papers, correspondence and, except as provided in paragraph 3 of article 31, his property, shall likewise enjoy inviolability.

Article 31

1. A diplomatic agent shall enjoy immunity from the criminal jurisdiction of the receiving State. He shall also enjoy immunity from its civil and administrative jurisdiction, except in the case of:

a. A real action relating to private immovable property situated in the territory of the receiving State, unless he holds it on behalf of the sending State for the purposes of the mission;
b. An action relating to succession in which the diplomatic agent is involved as executor, administrator, heir or legatee as a private person and not on behalf of the sending State;
c. An action relating to any professional or commercial activity exercised by the diplomatic agent in the receiving State outside his official functions.

2. A diplomatic agent is not obliged to give evidence as a witness.

3. No measures of execution may be taken in respect of a diplomatic agent except in the cases coming under subparagraphs (*a*), (*b*) and (*c*) of paragraph 1 of this article, and provided that the measures concerned can be

taken without infringing the inviolability of his person or of his residence.

4. The immunity of a diplomatic agent from the jurisdiction of the receiving State does not exempt him from the jurisdiction of the sending State.

Article 32

1. The immunity from jurisdiction of diplomatic agents and of persons enjoying immunity under article 37 may be waived by the sending State.

2. Waiver must always be express.

3. The initiation of proceedings by a diplomatic agent or by a person enjoying immunity from jurisdiction under article 37 shall preclude him from invoking immunity from jurisdiction in respect of any counterclaim directly connected with the principal claim.

4. Waiver of immunity from jurisdiction in respect of civil or administrative proceedings shall not be held to imply waiver of immunity in respect of the execution of the judgement, for which a separate waiver shall be necessary.

Article 33

1. Subject to the provisions of paragraph 3 of this article, a diplomatic agent shall with respect to services rendered for the sending State be exempt from social security provisions which may be in force in the receiving State.

2. The exemption provided for in paragraph 1 of this article shall also apply to private servants who are in the sole employ of a diplomatic agent, on condition:

a. That they are not nationals of or permanently resident in the receiving State; and

b. That they are covered by the social security provisions which may be in force in the sending State or a third State.

3. A diplomatic agent who employs persons to whom the exemption provided for in paragraph 2 of this article does not apply shall observe the obligations which the social security provisions of the receiving State impose upon employers.

4. The exemption provided for in paragraphs 1 and 2 of this article shall not preclude voluntary participation in the social security system of the receiving State provided that such participation is permitted by that State.

5. The provisions of this article shall not affect bilateral or multilateral agreements concerning social security concluded previously and shall not prevent the conclusion of such agreements in the future.

Article 34

A diplomatic agent shall be exempt from all dues and taxes, personal or real, national, regional or municipal, except:

a. Indirect taxes of a kind which are normally incorporated in the price of goods or services;

b. Dues and taxes on private immovable property situated in the territory of the receiving State, unless he holds it on behalf of the sending State for the purposes of the mission;

c. Estate, succession or inheritance duties levied by the receiving State, subject to the provisions of paragraph 4 of article 39;

d. Dues and taxes on private income having its source in the receiving State and capital taxes on investments made in commercial undertakings in the receiving State;

e. Charges levied for specific services rendered;

f. Registration, court or record fees, mortgage dues and stamp duty, with respect to immovable property, subject to the provisions of article 23.

Article 35

The receiving State shall exempt diplomatic agents from all personal services, from all public service of any kind whatsoever, and from military obligations such as those connected with requisitioning, military contributions and billeting.

Article 36

1. The receiving State shall, in accordance with such laws and regulations as it may adopt, permit entry of and grant exemption from all customs duties, taxes, and related charges other than charges for storage, cartage and similar services, on:

a. Articles for the official use of the mission;
b. Articles for the personal use of a diplomatic agent or members of his family forming part of his household, including articles intended for his establishment.

2. The personal baggage of a diplomatic agent shall be exempt from inspection, unless there are serious grounds for presuming that it contains articles not covered by the exemptions mentioned in paragraph 1 of this article, or articles the import or export of which is prohibited by the law or controlled by the quarantine regulations of the receiving State. Such inspection shall be conducted only in the presence of the diplomatic agent or of his authorized representative.

Article 37

1. The members of the family of a diplomatic agent forming part of his household shall, if they are not nationals of the receiving State, enjoy the privileges and immunities specified in articles 29 to 36.

2. Members of the administrative and technical staff of the mission, together with members of their families forming part of their respective households, shall, if they are not nationals of orpermanently resident in the receiving State, enjoy the privileges and immunities specified in articles 29 to 35, except that the immunity from civil and administrative jurisdiction of the receiving State specified in paragraph 1 of article 31 shall not extend to acts performed outside the course of their duties. They shall also enjoy the privileges specified in article 36, paragraph 1, in respect of articles imported at the time of first installation.

3. Members of the service staff of the mission who are not nationals of or permanently resident in the receiving State shall enjoy immunity in respect of acts performed in the course of their duties, exemption from dues and taxes on the emoluments they receive by reason of their employment and the exemption contained in article 33.

4. Private servants of members of the mission shall, if they are not nationals of or permanently resident in the receiving State, be exempt from dues and taxes on the emoluments they receive by reason of their employment. In other respects, they may enjoy privileges and immunities only to the extent admitted by the receiving State. However, the receiving State must exercise its jurisdiction over those persons in such a manner as not to interfere unduly with the performance of the functions of the mission.

Article 38

1. Except insofar as additional privileges and immunities may be granted by the receiving State, a diplomatic agent who is a national of or permanently resident in that State shall enjoy only immunity from jurisdiction, and inviolability, in respect of official acts performed in the exercise of his functions.

2. Other members of the staff of the mission and private servants who are nationals of or permanently resident in the receiving State shall enjoy privileges and immunities only to the extent admitted by the receiving State. However, the receiving State must exercise its jurisdiction over those persons in such a manner as not to interfere unduly with the performance of the functions of the mission.

Article 39

1. Every person entitled to privileges and immunities shall enjoy them from the moment he enters the territory of the receiving State on proceeding to take up his post or, if already in its territory, from the moment when his appointment is notified to the Ministry for Foreign Affairs or such other ministry as may be agreed.

2. When the functions of a person enjoying privileges and immunities have come to an end, such privileges and immunities shall normally cease at the moment when he leaves the country, or on expiry of a reasonable period in which to do so, but shall subsist until that time, even in case of armed conflict. However, with respect to acts

performed by such a person in the exercise of his functions as a member of the mission, immunity shall continue to subsist.

3. In case of the death of a member of the mission, the members of his family shall continue to enjoy the privileges and immunities to which they are entitled until the expiry of a reasonable period in which to leave the country.

4. In the event of the death of a member of the mission not a national of or permanently resident in the receiving State or a member of his family forming part of his household, the receiving State shall permit the withdrawal of the movable property of the deceased, with the exception of any property acquired in the country the export of which was prohibited at the time of his death. Estate, succession and inheritance duties shall not be levied on movable property the presence of which in the receiving State was due solely to the presence there of the deceased as a member of the mission or as a member of the family of a member of the mission.

Article 40

1. If a diplomatic agent passes through or is in the territory of a third State, which has granted him a passport visa if such visa was necessary, while proceeding to take up or to return to his post, or when returning to his own country, the third State shall accord him inviolability and such other immunities as may be required to ensure his transit or return. The same shall apply in the case of any members of his family enjoying privileges or immunities

who are accompanying the diplomatic agent, or travelling separately to join him or to return to their country.

2. In circumstances similar to those specified in paragraph 1 of this article, third States shall not hinder the passage of members of the administrative and technical or service staff of a mission, and of members of their families, through their territories.

3. Third States shall accord to official correspondence and other official communications in transit, including messages in code or cipher, the same freedom and protection as is accorded by the receiving State. They shall accord to diplomatic couriers, who have been granted a passport visa if such visa was necessary, and diplomatic bags in transit, the same inviolability and protection as the receiving State is bound to accord.

4. The obligations of third States under paragraphs 1, 2 and 3 of this article shall also apply to the persons mentioned respectively in those paragraphs, and to official communications and diplomatic bags, whose presence in the territory of the third State is due to force majeure.

Article 41

1. Without prejudice to their privileges and immunities, it is the duty of all persons enjoying such privileges and immunities to respect the laws and regulations of the receiving State. They also have a duty not to interfere in the internal affairs of that State.

2. All official business with the receiving State entrusted to the mission by the sending State shall be conducted with

or through the Ministry for Foreign Affairs of the receiving State or such other ministry as may be agreed.

3. The premises of the mission must not be used in any manner incompatible with the functions of the mission as laid down in the present Convention or by other rules of general international law or by any special agreements in force between the sending and the receiving State.

Article 42

A diplomatic agent shall not in the receiving State practise for personal profit any professional or commercial activity.

Article 43

The function of a diplomatic agent comes to an end, inter alia:

a. On notification by the sending State to the receiving State that the function of the diplomatic agent has come to an end;

b. On notification by the receiving State to the sending State that, in accordance with paragraph 2 of article 9, it refuses to recognize the diplomatic agent as a member of the mission.

Article 44

The receiving State must, even in case of armed conflict, grant facilities in order to enable persons enjoying privileges and immunities, other than nationals of the receiving State, and members of the families of such persons irrespective of their nationality, to leave at the earliest possible moment. It must, in particular, in case of need, place at their disposal the necessary means of transport for themselves and their property.

Article 45

If diplomatic relations are broken off between two States, or if a mission is permanently or temporarily recalled:

a. The receiving State must, even in case of armed conflict, respect and protect the premises of the mission, together with its property and archives;

b. The sending State may entrust the custody of the premises of the mission, together with its property and archives, to a third State acceptable to the receiving State;

c. The sending State may entrust the protection of its interests and those of its nationals to a third State acceptable to the receiving State.

Article 46

A sending State may with the prior consent of a receiving State, and at the request of a third State not represented in the receiving State, undertake the temporary protection of the interests of the third State and of its nationals.

Article 47

1. In the application of the provisions of the present Convention, the receiving State shall not discriminate as between States.

2. However, discrimination shall not be regarded as taking place:

a. Where the receiving State applies any of the provisions of the present Convention restrictively because of a restrictive application of that provision to its mission in the sending State;

b. Where by custom or agreement States extend to each other more favourable treatment than is required by the provisions of the present Convention.

Article 48

The present Convention shall be open for signature by all States Members of the United Nations or of any of the specialized agencies Parties to the Statute of the International Court of Justice, and by any other State invited by the General Assembly of the United Nations to become a Party to the Convention, as follows: until 31 October 1961 at the Federal Ministry for Foreign Affairs of Austria and subsequently, until 31 March 1962, at the United Nations Headquarters in New York.

Article 49

The present Convention is subject to ratification. The instruments of ratification shall be deposited with the Secretary-General of the United Nations.

Article 50

The present Convention shall remain open for accession by any State belonging to any of the four categories mentioned in article 48. The instruments of accession shall be deposited with the Secretary-General of the United Nations.

Article 51

1. The present Convention shall enter into force on the thirtieth day following the date of deposit of the twenty-second instrument of ratification or accession with the Secretary-General of the United Nations.

2. For each State ratifying or acceding to the Convention after the deposit of the twenty-second instrument of ratification or accession, the Convention shall enter into force on the thirtieth day after deposit by such State of its instrument of ratification or accession.

Article 52

The Secretary-General of the United Nations shall inform all States belonging to any of the four categories mentioned in article 48:

a. Of signatures to the present Convention and of the deposit of instruments of ratification or accession, in accordance with articles 48, 49 and 50;

b. Of the date on which the present Convention will enter into force, in accordance with article 51.

Article 53

The original of the present Convention, of which the Chinese, English, French, Russian and Spanish texts are equally authentic, shall be deposited with the Secretary-General of the United Nations, who shall send certified copies thereof to all States belonging to any of the four categories mentioned in article 48.

IN WITNESS WHEREOF the undersigned Plenipotentiaries, being duly authorized thereto by their respective Governments, have signed the present Convention.

DONE at Vienna this eighteenth day of April one thousand nine hundred and sixty-one.

www.ingramcontent.com/pod-product-compliance
Lightning Source LLC
LaVergne TN
LVHW022045200926
848481LV00003B/792